APOCALYPTIC VISIONS
PAST AND PRESENT

APOCALYPTIC VISIONS
PAST AND PRESENT

Selected Papers from the Eighth and Ninth
Annual Florida State University
Conferences on Literature and Film

Edited by JoAnn James
and William J. Cloonan

UNIVERSITY PRESSES OF FLORIDA

THE FLORIDA STATE UNIVERSITY PRESS
TALLAHASSEE

UNIVERSITY PRESSES OF FLORIDA is the central agency for scholarly publishing of the State of Florida's university system, producing books selected for publication by the faculty editorial committees of Florida's nine public universities: Florida A&M University (Tallahassee), Florida Atlantic University (Boca Raton), Florida International University (Miami), Florida State University (Tallahassee), University of Central Florida (Orlando), University of Florida (Gainesville), University of North Florida (Jacksonville), University of South Florida (Tampa), University of West Florida (Pensacola).

ORDERS for books published by all member presses of University Presses of Florida should be addressed to University Presses of Florida, 15 NW 15th Street, Gainesville, FL 32603

Library of Congress Cataloging-in-Publication Data
Florida State University Conference on Literature and
     Film (8th : 1983 : 9th : 1984 : Tallahassee, Fla.)
     Apocalyptic visions past and present.

     "A Florida State University Book."
     Includes index.
     1. Motion pictures and literature—Congresses. 2. Apocalyptic literature—History and criticism—Congresses. 3. Apocalypse in motion pictures—Congresses. I. James, JoAnn. II. Cloonan, William J. III. Florida State University Conference on Literature and Film (9th : 1984 : Tallahassee, Fla.). IV. Title.
PN1995.3.F55 1983   791.43' 09'   09353—dc 19
ISBN 0-8130-0894-8 : $12.00   87–29528 CIP

CONTENTS

ACKNOWLEDGMENTS

The authors and all those associated with the organization of the conferences generating this collection of papers express their appreciation to Augustus B. Turnbull, Provost of the Florida State University, for his continuing support of the conferences, and to Werner A. Baum, Dean of the College of Arts and Sciences of Florida State University, for helping financially to make this volume possible. We are also indebted to the Departments of Classics, English, and Modern Languages and Linguistics of the Florida State University for their backing of the conferences. Many people have helped the editors in the preparation of this volume, but we would like to give particular thanks to Florida State University Press production editor Hope Kurtz and to her assistants Scott Judy, Rebecca de Neve, Howard George, Kathleen Laufenberg, Audrey Cason, and Julie Wood, without whose editorial assistance and production work the publication of this volume would not have been possible.

— J. J. and W. J. C.

1. INTRODUCTION: APOCALYPTIC VISIONS PAST AND PRESENT

JoAnn James

APOCALYPTIC VISIONS HAVE long been the privileged domain of mystics and madmen, poets and prophets, apostles and apostates. Janus-like, the apocalyptic vision gazes behind and beyond the present moment, binding in an eternal future perfect cataclysmic conclusions and beginnings—the Harrowing of Hell and Eternity in a grain of sand. Flourishing in the historical watershed of 200 B.C.–200 A.D. when the anarchy of European tribal cultures and the intrigues of the princelings of the Middle East were falling alike before the oncoming juggernaut of the *Pax Romana*, apocalyptic literature served as encouragement and consolation in an age of crisis and telic inspiration, linking the end of one vision of man to the birth of a new World Child, the old order of blood and iron to a vision of infinite peace.

Although Jewish apocalyptic literature of the period was dominated by the perspective of catastrophe—the fall of Jerusalem and the sacking of the Temple of Herod by Titus occurred in 70 A.D.— Roman and Christian writers, inhabitants of the new era, envisaged a period of harmony and justice assured by the political triumph of the empire or the spiritual triumph of the Kingdom. Both traditions are encompassed in the best known of all apocalyptic texts, the last canonical book of the New Testament, *The Apocalypse of John the Apostle,* in which the visions vouchsafed by the angel to John of Patmos explode into symbolic language and the archetypal imagery of nightmare.

1

The maelstroms of the twentieth century have given contemporary urgency to a new apocalyptic literature. The pounding hoofbeats of the Four Horsemen thunder not only across Africa, India, and the nations of the Middle East but into our bedrooms, "between the desire and the spasm." If we cannot name the horror that lurks at the heart of our darkness, it is because its name is legion. Whether with a bang or whimper, annihilation beckons to man and mankind.

There are, however, other possibilities of "apocalyptic visions." In the most recent translations of the *New Testament, The Apocalypse of John the Apostle* is called *The Book of Revelation.* The change of title reflects more than the linguistic and theological popularizations of the new evangelism. The Greek verb αποκαλυπτειν means to uncover, to disclose, to reveal. Neither classical Greek literature nor the Septuagint associate the term with cosmic upheavals. What is laid bare may provide a revelation—a new way of seeing, experiencing, knowing. It can occur as readily in the extended handclasp of Miss Lonelyhearts and Doyle as on the killing fields of Nordhausen.

The present collection of essays, which contains selected papers from the Eighth and Ninth Annual Conferences on Literature and Film held at Florida State University, is therefore not limited to the discussion of works emerging from experience of warfare and mass slaughter. The editors have endeavored to balance catastrophe with revelation. In each of the essays chosen, the critic demonstrates the rhetorical or contextual means by which the author/cinematographer moves beyond the particular incident or moment toward a revelation of more profound significance.

∞

Although the surface of the text may present itself in apparent nudity to the scrutiny of every eye, there is more to "l'affaire litéraire" than meets the eye. The text, be it verbal, iconographic or cinematographic, is double—obscure and transparent, concealing and disclosing. It comprises "un secret, la chose à dissimuler," as Derrida states. The critical task demands therefore not interface but penetration. If the critic has ceased to be the mystagogue, he retains the authority of privileged connoisseur, a reader of particular "literary competency" whose quest is the interrogation of the text, open-

2

ing its hermetic fastness to dialogue through which it can be better known and enjoyed.

Does the rough beast now slouch toward Bethlehem or Brazil to give birth? Michael Popkin's essay on George Steiner's controversial novel *The Portage to San Cristóbal of A.H.* (1981) demonstrates that the "paradoxical and ambiguous narrative" of the novel is the result of Steiner's conscious manipulation of "two different and even mutually exclusive genres" within the text: the Holocaust novel (e.g., *The Last of the Just)* and the "thriller" (e.g., *The Boys from Brazil)*—a technique Popkin successfully duplicates by playing off a "thriller," Len Deighton's *XPD,* against *Portage.* Hitler's concluding (although far from conclusive) speech of self-defense ends by evoking the final day of judgment and revelation which in the apocalyptic tradition separates the historical age of catastrophe from the prophesied age of peace: "and in the midst of incertitude must matters be left till the great revelation of all secrets." The hovering helicopters whose noise precludes further speech provide an ironically arbitrary conclusion in which are interwoven Judaism's thunder-voiced god, the wings of the eagle which are to return the faithful from their exile to Jerusalem, and the dragon chariot of Greek tragedy, *dei ex machina* all.

However, Popkin argues, the real issue that emerges from *Portage* has little to do with the degree of Hitler's responsibility for the massacre of the Jews. Language and its inability to communicate are the author's true subjects. The subversive narrative strategy of confronting two genres—the "serious" novel and the "thriller," which undermine and "unwrite" each other until they converge and noise triumphs—is the final revelation of the impotence of language. Despite the presence within the novel of a character named Benasseraf, whose name evokes both scribe and angel (fusing the functions of both John and his divine messenger), no "vision" can be transmitted because his work *Le silence et le poète* represents a negation of communication: if the "maker" does not create how shall he be the "maker," and the work itself, although "tenaciously projected," is unwritten.

And what of Teku, the Amazon native "come out of Eden"? The only non-Jew present at Hitler's trial for genocide, Teku can hear but is incapable of understanding what is said at the trial because its language is unknown to him. Is he even aware of the rape of the Amazon and the genocide of the Amazon Indians being carried out before his eyes? Silent witnesses, like silent poets, are impotent. Is Brazil new Eden or anti-Eden? Shall we expect from it a Second Coming—son, minion, clone—or only Teku, a second Adam? Popkin stirs us to question and debate.

∞

And after Armageddon? The successive conflicts of the twentieth century have most egregiously failed to lead us to the paths of glory. Neither by force of arms nor by moral integrity has Everyman broken through to triumphant apotheosis. In "Wyndham Lewis's *The Childermass* (1928): The Slaughter of the Innocents in the Age of Cinema," Paul Tiessen discusses Lewis's use of cinema as a metaphor for a new genocide, its techniques as correlative of our social and spiritual alienation.

The Childermass, ritual mourning for how many massacres, how many innocents, illustrates the malaise of "l'homme moyen sensuel." In Lewis's surreal, evanescent afterworld, Year One finds two "hollow men," Pulley: Satters (Didi: Gogo), walking upon a beach amid a crowd of transients, some insubstantial as Homer's chattering specters. They await transportation across the river (of a thousand names, nameless here) to the Magnetic City that flickers on the farther shore, girt with mighty mountains, the whole infused by an "apocalyptic coloration." From time to time a *son et lumière* spectacle heralds the arrival of the Phoenix. The illuminated city wall radiates strength and majesty. Presiding over spectator and spectacle is a deprecatory Bailiff (of Oz?).

Tiessen demonstrates that despite the wealth of detail, Lewis uses cinematographic techniques as a subversive narrative strategy, undermining and distorting the objective existence of what he has described, leading to an endless distancing of "reality." If the mountains, archetypal symbol of Permanence linking Heaven, Earth and Hell, ladder of man's ascent and God's descent, are only "pukka" (cardboard) mountains, based on the mountains of Iceland; if the "Magnetic City" is but a cut of Griffith's Babylon; if the Phoenix, Christian symbol of the Resurrection as well as that of the individual, is a stuffed bird upon a string; if the Ancient of Sinai dwells not in the "pukka" mountains but on this bank and wears the Bailiff's cap—there is no sure ground. Everything is immeasurably less than we had hoped. Massman enslaved by the manipulation of media images passively waits until he flickers out. No need for the delicate monster to soil itself with further bloodshed; the new generation of innocents will pass gently into death's other kingdom.

∞

Harry Rosser also explores the use of cinematographic techniques in his discussion of Carlos Fuentes's novel, *The Death of Artemio Cruz*. Acknowledging Fuentes's abandonment of "the vulgarity of plausible concatenation," in Beckett's phrase, his repeated subversion of narrative conventions by arbitrary juxtapositions, conflicting confirmations and subtle contradictions, shifting narrative perspectives and transposed chronologies, Rosser sets as his critical aim "giving meaning to a text that initially does not make sense." Together with the dying protagonist, he seeks to construct meanings—aspirations, behavior, consequence—from the chaos of events.

Like Sartre's condemned Spanish revolutionary in *Le Mur,* Cruz would "understand" before dying: "Je ne voulais pas crever comme une bête. Je voulais comprendre." In constructing his own past, Cruz also traces the course of the Mexican revolution. With him we follow this *via crucis.*

For Artemio, the first fall from idealistic authenticity is caused by the death of Regina. Abandoning Gonzalo, the pure revolutionary, Cruz reenacts abandonment of the revolution by its leaders, betrayal upon betrayal. Gonzalo finds ironic and absurd continuity in the unblinking watcher at Cruz's side, the dying man's wife, Gonzalo's sister, Catalina. His ideals, although betrayed by Cruz, are reborn in Cruz's son Lorenzo, who dies in the Spanish Civil War.

Accepting at last, as Rosser argues, responsibility for the past with its sordid betrayal, permits Cruz to assume pride in Lorenzo's ideals and self-sacrifice. Past and present coalesce to give birth to a new future of different potential. Final remembrance and acceptance of the past liberate the *fabula* from discoherent discourse and Artemio from the contingencies of existence. He can now die at peace "Tel qu'en lui-même enfin l'éternité le change."

∞

Kurosawa's epic film *Kagemusha* depicts the clash of feudal warlords in medieval Japan, culminating in the Battle of Nagashino in 1575. Beyond the splendor of the historical pageantry played against a landscape of mountains and forests a personal drama unfolds within Lord Takeda's stronghold: a captured thief, double of Takeda, assumes the warlord's domestic and public roles.

John Gourlie's essay on the film, "War and Pastoral: The Treatment of Landscape and Value in Kurosawa's *Kagemusha*," is concerned with neither political nor domestic drama but rather with Kurosawa's achievement in using visual imagery as the objective correlative of ideas, emotions, and values. The archetypal landscape —mountain, forest, river, lake, wind—imparts mythic significance to the historical moment. Emblazoned on the banners of the samurai, these symbols transform the men who bear them into elemental natural forces.

Two images, as Gourlie demonstrates, dominate the landscape—mountain and water. Takeda's banner is the mountain, his castle a mountain fortress, his battle station a raised throne whence, impassive as the mountain, he watches the battle surge forward. To leave his natural element and descend into the plain is his hubristic mortal error. Although the mountain's mass indicates its symbolic value of permanence, it is subject to erosion, its face eventually dissolved into sand and tumbling pebbles.

Water plays an ambiguous role in the film. The castle must have an assured water supply; the lake serves as tomb for the secret burial of Takeda, and as womb from which the thief is reborn as hero in the film's concluding moments. The river delimits Takeda's domain and quite literally separates this world from the next for, when a new leader replaces Takeda's *tanist*, he leads his troops across the water to a final doomed encounter. In the apocalyptic final image, the one samurai and his banner are borne away by the river.

∞

The symbiotic relationship between the individual and his environment as manifested in the novels and autobiography of Thomas Hardy is the subject of Fran E. Chalfont's essay, "Kindly Congruity: Utopian and Dystopian Elements in Hardy's Life and Works." Within the major novels, Chalfont discerns a triptych of archetypal settings which coincide closely with Frye's system of correspondences between the seasons of year, plot phases, and stylistic mode. These three major settings, all familiar to Hardy from his childhood,

6

comprise Egdon Heath, the Vale of the Great Dairies, and Flint-combe-Ash Farm.

Egdon Heath, setting for *The Return of the Native,* "a vast tract of unenclosed wild," is far from the conventional beauty of the English countryside. "Darkest vegetation" grows in somber rounds and hollows beneath a darkening sky; the heath itself seems to be "exhaling darkness." The whole is "slighted and enduring; and withal singularly colossal and mysterious in its swarthy monotony." This is the landscape of the unconscious—it offers womblike security for those "in harmony with its spirit."

The second and third panels of this landscape occur in *Tess of the d'Urbervilles.* The Edenic Vale of the Great Dairies corresponds to the "summer phase" of Frye's schema, the period of triumph, possession, sacred marriage. All is golden sunshine and green hedgerows, clear air and water. The fields teem with fat and fertile kine, and Tess is loved by the "god-like" summer king, Angel. But the promise of happiness is not fulfilled. The separation of Tess and Angel propels her into the bleak "winter phase" of disappointment and despair. Hardy furnishes as correlative landscape the wasteland, or blasted heath. The land surrounding Flintcombe-Ash is "a desolate drab" with grotesque outcroppings of white phallic flint like misshapen gravestones. Out of the winding sheets of snow swirl birds, archetypal messengers of the gods, whose "eyes had witnessed scenes of cataclysmal horror." But the potential message is silenced—they bring no tidings.

In *Jude the Obscure,* Chalfont illustrates a new use of landscape which fulfills a dramatic function in the novel, the destruction of the ancient beauty and harmony of the English countryside now prey to progress and prosperity. The "new-old cultural disjunction" is manifest in Marygreen where the ancient church has been torn down and recycled as "pig-sty walls, garden seats ... and rockeries in the flower beds of the neighborhood." Its replacement, conceived of no time or culture, is "modern Gothic." Shaston's "near mythical Anglo-Saxon and medieval glories" are shunned by the modern inhabitants who prefer their circuses and sideshows. However, though the architectural and aesthetic values may have been debased and distorted, it is plain that on the social level the bastions are undisturbed—the self-taught dray-boy will never attend tutorials in the shadows of the "turrets and spires of Christminster."

The full discongruity of man and environment occurs when the country dweller abandons his rural homestead for the Victorian ghettos of the working class, "row lives in row houses." This is the setting that spawns Hardy's most terrifying and original visions: the city as monster, its myriad glass panes (Crystal Palaces?) reflecting the coldness of the winter sun and the crowd as a multi-limbed beast with an eye in each pore of its vast body. From landscape as womb-like protection to devouring mythic monster, Chalfont has demonstrated Hardy's prophetic vision of twentieth-century urban life: overpopulated, alienated, crime-ridden, anonymous, devouring.

∞

One's first recollection of Voltaire's *Candide* is likely to be a montage of amassed natural catastrophes—famine, drought, earthquake, and clips of man's brutality to man—slavery, auto-da-fé, public executions; rather similar to any evening's romp through T.V. land. "Childhood's End: Apocalyptic Resolution in *Candide*" is concerned with the other side of the narrative—with the tension between episodic horrors and the repetition of the thematic image of the garden.

The gardens of *Candide* are multiple and contribute significantly to the total resonance of the work. To fail to consider their contribution to the narrative is to equate Voltaire's view with that of Martin, the Manichean pessimist, and reduce life's perspective to unmitigated horror. In each garden, from Westphalie to the *métairie,* the discordant element is man. If man and the earth he lives upon and from are adversaries—man enslaved to the soil he tills—then all labor is exploitation and Genesis's curse is fulfilled. The contrary is also considered—in boundlessly rich Eldorado man's activity is futile; none of its inhabitants need ever move from silken cushions. It is the Pascalian dilemma: without *divertissements*, man is alone with mortality and madness is the exit.

However, following stepping-stone gardens scattered amid the carnage, Candide finds eventually both his own garden and himself. The famous concluding line of the text is thus shown to be not an airy, arbitrary resolution to a tale of horror, a neat bandage to a gangrenous wound, but a reconciliation between man and man as well as man and earth, permitting each to flourish through communal labor. Now, Candide-man can look upon the earth and the fruit of his labors and find that it is good.

8

In her essay *"India Song/Le Vice-Consul* of Marguerite Duras: Comparative Techniques in Film and Novel," Patricia Struebig utilizes novel, screen text and film as confronting, contradicting, and complementary texts. Her aim is to assess varying audience perception of the Vice-Consul's "story," different versions of which occur in five of Duras's works. She is concerned with both the similarities and differences among the versions as she searches for a meaning perhaps deliberately obscured.

As Struebig notes, Anne-Marie Stretter and the Vice-Consul appear in no less than three novels and two films of Duras in the decade 1964–74, all of them dealing with the same love story, variations on the multiple facets of love. Although the novels pinpoint subtle details more precisely, certain emotional values are more efficiently and sensitively evoked by auditory imagery—particularly the musical leit-motif—and others by visual images such as flux and reflux of the dancing figures or the misery of the massed beggars and lepers.

It is ultimately the film which permits us "to understand" the story by participating through the camera's eye in the experience of India whose heat, clamor, lepers, and beggars exist with an intensity upon the screen that verbal description does not approach. The speed of the camera, broken phrases, and repetition impose upon the eye the morbid "ennui" of the main characters and permit the viewer to recognize in Anne-Marie Stretter and the Vice-Consul the confronting and complementary values of the "Two into One," the Yin and Yang of the inextricably bound forces of Life and Death, providing mythic dimension to what might have been a banal incident.

∞

The rainbow, symbol of catastrophic endings—the destruction of the world by water, as well as symbol of a new age and new hope of redemption—gives a manic mythic significance to Thomas Pynchon's novel *Gravity's Rainbow.* The scimitar span of the rainbow, here identified with the trajectory of a V-2 rocket, is also a sword of Damocles, threatening imminent destruction as the price of a second failure. Laurence Daw's discussion of the novel, "The Apocalyptic Milieu of Pynchon's *Gravity's Rainbow,*" points to this dual role of the novel as apocalyptic and post-apocalyptic, and speculates that the nature of such literature is inherently romantic. Pyn-

9

chon's view of the world, Daw argues, is the balance between horror and limitless beauty, destruction and redemption, bound together as in the text of St. John.

This view permits a radical reinterpretation of our familiar icons—the atomic bomb's ironic White Angel mushroom transmuted into a "giant white cock, dangling in the sky straight downward out of a white pubic bush." Against the aerodynamic designers of death, Pynchon weighs the value of love—the pastoral idyll of Jessica and Roger Mexico, and the life force of Slothrop's dream—the fecundity of the earth mother womb that recreates all species. The *Raketen-Stadt*, in whose trash-littered gardens lurks the serpent hourobouros tempting man to create new substances, and Mingeborough maintain a perilous equilibrium. Ombindi and the Empty Ones seek "the Final Zero"—individual and racial annihilation. Enzian preaches "the Eternal Center"—without history, eternity, and peace. Is this the moment for Voltaire's Vieille to ask the overwhelming question? In the meantime, an ironic stability is attained as both groups cooperate on the newest death toy, Rocket 00001. In conclusion, Daw argues that although the novel ends with the explosion of Rocket 00000, its final unfinished phrase provides a potential for reversal. "Pynchon would have us recreate the fallen world and ascend to the realm of timeless Being of the Angels." *Pace, Pascal.*

∞

In "Metonymy and Psychological Realism in Autobiography," R. Victoria Arana challenges some prevalent assumptions concerning authorial identity in autobiography, distinguishing the "implied" from the historal author. Since reader acceptance of this genre demands faith in its "realism," she investigates what constitutes an impression of psychological realism. Metonymy, which demands the participation of the reader and cannot function without the reader's ability to furnish context for the term chosen, is a successful rhetorical device because of its power to simplify and intensify vision. It may also reify emotion and subjective values. We are convinced of the reality of what is so presented on the basis of our own experiences. For Arana authorial control of such a figure is axiomatic; all images are invested with intention and refusing to admit this sabotages the pleasure of the text.

Turning to Boris Pasternak's autobiography, *Safe Conduct,* Arana examines two passages whose total emotional power is derived from the use of metonymy and proves that these passages simultaneously create the illusion of realism by bringing the reader into direct participation with the text while at the same time they also serve to distance the author from the scene, making him unknown and unknowable. She concludes that implied author and historical author coincide only on the basis of their literary craftsmanship. Our vision of the work, the artist, and "reality" must ultimately depend upon the sensitivity and respect with which we approach the stylistic analysis of any given text.

∞

The concluding essay in this collection, Walter Poznar's "The Apocalyptic Vision of Nathanael West's *Miss Lonelyhearts,*" focuses on the tragedy of human existence in twentieth century America. West's tragic vision presents the world as ashen waste, the individual as an alienated and violent being, spiritually barren, sodden with cheap dreams. The secular faiths of the modern age—eighteenth–century optimism in social and technological progress, nineteenth–century pursuit of wealth and the twentieth–century lust for global power—no longer energize the soul. Lacking both the courage to affirm and the strength to deny, the "busy monster mankind" can be neither hero nor villain of our tale.

But what of the "outsider?" For the Miss Lonelyhearts, Poznar concludes, the modern world affords no retreat—nature is a heap of rotting leaves hiding gray and white fungi; the past age of heroes is beyond our comprehension. (Miss Lonelyhearts may suffer for mankind as Prometheus in the heroic age, but times have transmogrified the rending eagle into the pecking Shrike.) Ironic detachment is impossible for those who feel the hedonistic life productive of ever-increasing physical and spiritual malaise. If the protagonist is the Man of Sorrows condemned to absorb the pitiful anguish and pain distilled into the letters he receives from countless pathetic people, there is still possible communication and communion. The clasped hands of Doyle and Lonelyhearts move beyond mere gesture.

What redeems West's bleak vision, in Poznar's evaluation, is that he refused the facile cynicism and sophisticated detachment of

11

his contemporaries, battling his own demons of disbelief and madness to witness "the vast agony of the world" while retaining an "unshakable and clear-sighted respect for man."

∞

All of the essays included here deal with revelation, understanding, new perception. The topic is the human condition, the terrors that stalk us, the stubborn hope that persists, the debasement of our dreams and the courage to formulate new ones, and our pleasure amid chaos in the aesthetic contemplation of a film or a literary text. We have survived our catastrophes.

2. GEORGE STEINER'S
PORTAGE: HOLOCAUST
NOVEL OR THRILLER?

Michael Popkin

"YOU HEARD THE STORY about them finding
Hitler in São Paulo?" said Stein suddenly, his mouth
filled with chocolate and cherry. Everyone turned to
look at him. "They ask him to come back and run
Germany. No, he says, he won't go. So they keep
trying to persuade him. They bring in the public relations guys, and the ad agency men. They offer him
money and anything he wants." Stein looked round
to see if everyone was listening. They all were.
"Hitler says he likes it in São Paulo. He's got his
mortgage almost paid, and a grown-up son and a
married daughter by a second wife. He don't want
any part of going back to Germany. But finally he
gives in. But before he goes back to be dictator of
Germany again he insists on one thing . . . right!"
Stein waved a finger in the air in imitation of Hitler,
and hoarsely yelled, *"No more Mr. Nice Guy!"* Stein
laughed to show it was the punch line of the joke.
(Len Deighton, *XPD*)[1]

The Portage to San Cristóbal of A. H. by George Steiner
(1981), one of the most controversial novels of recent years, is

13

essentially a longer, more elaborate version of the same joke, but Steiner (unlike Stein) does not laugh at the end, and neither do his readers. In Steiner's narrative, a small band of Jews tracks down the ninety-year-old Adolf Hitler in a remote corner of the Amazonian jungle and struggles to carry him out into the cacophony and glare of the post-culture he helped create. This short novel has been most sharply criticized because it concludes with an eloquent speech by Hitler, in which he not only vindicates himself, but holds the Jews themselves ultimately responsible for the Holocaust. This speech of self-defense is particularly disturbing because Hitler's arguments are made to seem unanswerable by being given the final position in the novel. The reaction of Hyam Maccoby in *Encounter* may be cited as typical: "The result is . . . an upsetting and misleading piece of anti-Jewish propaganda of a regrettably contemporary kind which may prove to be of aid and comfort to anti-Semites for years to come."[2] A critic who attempts to defend Steiner, who himself fled from Hitler at an early age, from the incongruous charge of anti-Semitism, might assert either that the arguments offered by his Hitler are self-evidently unhistorical and specious, and therefore not to be taken seriously, or that the novel's ending is not really "final" at all.

My own contention is that *The Portage to San Cristóbal* is a mixture of two different and even mutually exclusive genres which are not combined so much as played off against one another until, at the novel's conclusion, they actually obliterate one another, revealing less about the causes of the Holocaust than about the nature of language.

One of Steiner's Jewish characters is a writer named G. Benasseraf who, like Steiner, has survived the holocaust and who reminisces about the glorious day when a study he published called *Le silence et le poète—Silence and the Poet*—was displayed in the window of the Libraire des Saint-Pères in Paris and lauded in *Le Monde*. Just when the reader recalls that Steiner himself has published a study called *Language and Silence,* the scene "perfectly framed"[3] in the mind of G. Benasseraf is revealed to be only a fantasy; *Silence and the Poet* is "unwritten though tenaciously projected" (68). G. Benasseraf is thus both a double for George Steiner and the anti-Steiner of unwritten books. As his name suggests, Benasseraf is both the son of a scribe and the son of an angel. This passage can be seen as the key to Steiner's text. Through Hitler's final speech, Steiner concludes the writing of his novel by unwriting the novel he has just written, in the familiar post-modernist manner of such writers as García Márquez and Thomas Pynchon, so that the reader seems to have completed a text like the one by Steiner's character, "unwritten though tenaciously projected," nonexistent but with a firmer hold on the imagination than many texts which exist in actuality.

Steiner's critics, by placing all their emphasis upon only one of the two genres he is setting in opposition, fail to grasp the manner in which one genre negates the other, thus turning a paradoxical and ambiguous narrative into a failed effort to do for Hitler what Milton did for Satan—give the devil his due. It is therefore not surprising that when Steiner's *Portage* is read in this way there will be critics to make the additional error also made with Milton—to see the writer as falling under the malign influence of his creation and giving the devil more than his due.

There is first something to be said about Hitler's arguments, which are perhaps not as objectionable out of context as they have been taken to be by the critics of this novel. Hitler's defense has four different articles: first, he asserts, the idea of "the chosen people" with "a promised land" was not a Nazi invention but an imitation: "My racism," Hitler tells his Jewish captors, "was a parody of yours" (164).

Second, Moses invented "an omnipotent, all-seeing, yet invisible, impalpable, inconceivable God," every jot of whose law must be obeyed; after Moses came Jesus and Marx, two more Jews who "demand of human beings more than they can give" and press upon mankind "the blackmail of transcendence" (164–66). Hitler's third point is that other mass murderers killed even *more* millions; "Stalin . . . slaughtered *thirty* million" and "perfected genocide when I was still a nameless scribbler in Munich" (168). As fourth and last point, it was the Holocaust that brought about the creation of the state of Israel, and therefore, in the long run, Hitler did the Jews a favor. Here, then, is Hitler's conclusion:

> "Gentleman of the tribunal: I took my doctrines from you. I fought the blackmail of the ideal with which you have hounded mankind. My crimes were matched and surpassed by those of others. The *Reich* begat Israel. These are my last words. The last words of a dying man against the last words of those

who suffered; and in the midst of incertitude must
matters be left till the great revelation of all secrets."
(170)

These arguments would never have entered the mind of the
historical Hitler, one feels sure, and the last two are almost totally
beside the point. On the other hand, it is surprising to find that
another of Steiner's critics called these four principles "for the most
part the stock-in-trade of conventional anti-Semitism."[4] Something
very close to the first two reasons Hitler gives here was argued by
Freud shortly before his death in 1939 in the essays published as
Moses and Monotheism, and Freud withheld their publication until
after he fled from Austria to England, not for fear of offending fellow Jews, but for fear of offending Hitler; as he explains, "lest my
publishing the book might cause psychoanalysis to be forbidden in a
country where its practice was still allowed."[5] The argument that
Jews are subconsciously hated by Gentiles for originating a higher
ethical standard and foisting it upon the Western world through the
intermediary of Christianity is developed at length by Leslie Fiedler
in his study *The Stranger in Shakespeare,* where even discounting
Fiedler's omnipresent references to "myth" and "archetype," what
remains is a very persuasive explication of *The Merchant of Venice.*
Finally, a much more elegantly argued version of the same idea is
presented by Steiner himself in his volume of lectures, *In Blue-
beard's Castle,* and Hitler's last two points are touched upon in
Language and Silence. This is not to suggest that Steiner agrees with
Hitler or that, as one critic rather intemperately puts it, "George
Steiner and Adolf Hitler become indistinguishable from one another"
(Plotinsky, 19). It should simply be noted that some of Hitler's arguments have been used by Jews themselves to explain anti-Semitism, although not, of course, to justify it. What is appalling in this
novel is less the speech than the speaker. The real issue is not how
true or false Hitler's arguments may be in the abstract, but why they
occupy the last ten pages of this novel and go unanswered.

If Hitler's arguments are not meant to sound patently absurd,
but logical enough to warrant some sort of response, why is there
no response in the novel? The most obvious reason is that the reader
is meant to work out the response individually, to enter into an open
argument rather than adjudicate a closed one. Steiner told an
interviewer, "I would like each individual to decide how he would

answer Hitler's defence."[6] Joseph Lowin has pointed to two other factors which contribute to the open nature of the conclusion: first is Teku, the "Indian guest come out of Eden," (157) the Amazon native who is the only non-Jewish spectator at Hitler's jungle trial and who leaps up to cry "Proved" after the defendant's speech, although "he had not understood the words, only their meaning" (170). Before the Indian can announce his verdict, however, or perhaps before he has finished crying it "to the earth twice and twice to the north as is the custom" (170), he is interrupted by the noise of helicopters. "The first helicopter was hovering above the clearing. The second"—and Steiner's novel ends in the middle of the sentence, with no punctuation. It is clear that this ending is self-consciously arbitrary, with the Indian's verdict not yet fully uttered and the only sound coming from what Lowin calls "the open-ended highly symbolic hovering of the helicopters."[7] Yet to say that Hitler does not *quite* have the last word, and that every reader has to formulate a personal response, thus turning Hitler's monologue into a dialogue, does not adequately deal with the forthright objection by John Leonard, whose review in the *New York Times* summed up Hitler's argument and added: "This, frankly, is obscene. Dostoyevsky didn't end *The Brothers Karamazov* with the tale of the Grand Inquisitor. Mr. Steiner, by choosing to end *The Portage* with something very much like that brutal rationalization (and by omitting the kiss), not only denies the power of art to arrange and transcend, but he makes me sick to my stomach."[8]

Somehow, given George Steiner's massively convincing credentials as both literary critic and humanist, it sounds even more damning to accuse him of being a bad artist than to accuse him of being an unconscious Nazi sympathizer. Is Steiner perhaps guilty after all—not of anti-Semitism but rather of hubris? In *Extraterritorial,* Steiner approvingly quoted Sartre's classic statement about the interrelationship between art and morality: "No one could suppose for an instant that it would be possible to write a good novel in praise of anti-Semitism."[9] If Steiner supposed for an instant that it would be possible to write a good novel that would praise anti-Semitism *temporarily,* to provoke a response by the reader, that response turned out to be outrage at an unjustifiable aesthetic gambit. To assert that *The Portage to San Cristóbal* does not really end with Hitler is finally no more satisfactory than to assert that it ends with rationalizations so patently specious that they need no refutation. A third way to defend the novel is to consider it in terms of reader response, which means to consider it as both Holocaust novel and as spy thriller.

It would be useful to have a more precise term than "spy thriller" for the kind of film that Alfred Hitchcock once directed in *The Man Who Knew Too Much* and *Saboteur,* and the kind of popular fiction being written now by such specialists in the genre as Len Deighton, Ken Follett, and Robert Ludlum. The term "mystery" has both metaphysical and detective connotations, and the favored term in England—"pulp"—sounds unnecessarily derogatory. "Thriller" seems most adequate to the purpose, even though Michael Jackson has temporarily preempted the term as a way to describe horror movies. In fact, the video of "Thriller" begins with a disclaimer in which Michael Jackson announces that his religious convictions prevent him from implying any belief in the garish supernatural events he is about to illustrate. That suggests a crucial distinction between the Holocaust novel and the spy thriller: a spy thriller uses the demons of Hitler and Nazi Germany the way a horror movie uses ghouls—to provoke pleasurable terror. While the Holocaust novel *The Last of the Just* ends with a section entitled "Never Again," the thriller's cry is "Ever Again," with Hitler, his minions, his sons, and his clones always ready to rise from the South American swampland to terrorize a new generation, but without any apparent moral significance. While Steiner's critics have made only an occasional, brief reference to spy thrillers—the reviewer in the *Times Literary Supplement,* for example, noted that "passages of kitsch are disconcertingly liable to surface"[10]—the structure of Steiner's novel cannot be fully understood in isolation from that genre. Alvin Rosenfeld, who wrote perhaps the best essay on *The Portage to San Cristóbal,* begins by noting that "with only a few exceptions (Hitler) has been almost entirely absent from contemporary literature"[11]—but he cannot be thinking of spy thrillers. Even a casual moviegoer has seen *Marathon Man* or *The Boys from Brazil,* and the idea that either Hitler or his symbolic equivalent lies ready to be resurrected, preferably in South America, is actually a staple of the kind of fiction I am discussing.

As a specific example I should like to use the spy thriller *XPD* by Len Deighton, which was published almost simultaneously with Steiner's *Portage* in 1981, thus eliminating any possibility of influence one way or the other, although such influence is scarcely likely. Len Deighton writes serious novels from time to time, and his previous work of fiction, *SS-GB,* was a convincingly detailed account of what England would have been like under a German occupation. *XPD* is one of Deighton's worst books, but as an example of the thriller genre it shows enough similarities to Steiner's *Portage* to establish a family resemblance.

In the first place, the basic thriller structure is to cut from one brief chapter to another, set somewhere else in the world, usually revealing the connection between these scenes only by an almost predictable ironic twist at the end of the chapter. So Steiner's *Portage* takes place in the Amazonian jungle, then London (final ironic twist: "the one they've caught is the double" [14]), then back to the jungle, then Moscow (final ironic twist, with the demon's name mentioned for the first time: "Hitler is alive" [39]), then back to the jungle, and so on, through Israel, Germany, France, Washington, D.C., and the steamy town of Orosso where a secret agent huddles over his shortwave radio. All of these characters, presumably, will converge on the jungle clearing where their various attitudes toward the reappearance of Hitler will produce some sort of confrontation and plot resolution—although, as I have already mentioned, it turns out that there will not be one. *XPD* moves from London to California to Moscow to Mexico in a similar manner, with agents from several different nations concerned not about Hitler exactly, but rather about a memorandum he once wrote which is about to resurface with dire consequences. One American explains, as the grand confrontation approaches, "It's not going to blow over, Colonel. We're fighting City Hall, don't you see that? The Brits and the Krauts both want the Hitler Minutes. If we don't let them have them, they'll blow us away. But if we *do* let them have them, they'll also blow us away" (260). Steiner's ending exactly, except that Len Deighton, needless to say, gives his readers this climactic scene. In each novel, the various characters and nations have their own reasons for not wanting Hitler or his mysterious documents to reappear. Steiner's Frenchman confides to his diary: "Even if the man they're dragging out of that jungle is still lucid, why open the old wounds? Things would get said, which all of us know. . . Do we really want that stuff pouring out all over the front pages once again, reminding us of our grosser indiscretions?" (140) Deighton's West German tells his colleagues, "Hitler is dead. . . . Let him remain dead. We want no revelations, no so-called Hitler Minutes, no secret plans to bring Hitler out of the grave and adorn him with the glories of newsworthy historical triumphs" (171). In Steiner, as in Deighton, the characters are all collections of genre clichés: the German loves classical music, the Frenchman has a demanding mistress, and so on. Here is part of a description of a British agent:

> He knew how to coax the metal prongs through the stiff paper in a Danish driving license so as not to betray a change of photograph. . . . He knew where the night express from Oporto, the 9:14, slowed down before entering Lisbon. He knew that the lack of proper lighting at the south end of the customs shed at Fishguard made it easy for a man to squat in the pools of shadow and wait for the tea break which came at 10:55 after the second ferry. Knowledge. Not the spindrift that fogs the minds of ordinary men. But nuggets, fine as Björnske ball bearings, and gathered at a price.

The most dedicated reader of thrillers would be hard put to guess the source of that quotation—it sounds more like Robert Ludlum at the edge of self-parody than like either of the writers under discussion —but it is George Steiner's description of Rodriguéz Kulken, master of borders and disguises (76) and it is genre writing that would serve any practitioner in the craft of spy thrillers. Another quotation will make the same point:

> [Hitler] was a shocking sight. . . . His face seemed to have aged forty years, his eye sockets were deeply sunken and the skin of his cheeks dark, as if bruised. He was stooped and seemed to have lost the use of his left arm, which trembled constantly. His voice was very low and hoarse and almost unrecognizable to anyone who had heard his speeches of earlier years—and which of us had not! When he spoke he leaned forward and used his right hand to grasp his throat, as if to help his vocal chords.

This particular passage is one that Steiner's readers might be quick to identify—but it comes from *XPD* by Len Deighton (102), which not only offers this Hitler in flashback, but the "Hitler-is-alive-in-South-America" joke which has already been quoted, and a spectacular final chase through a movie studio in which a thousand actors, all in costume, are auditioning for the role of Hitler in a movie (301–3). In the closest he comes to presenting a serious theme seriously, Deighton offers the growing friendship between an aging Jewish-American who fought with the Allied forces during the Second World War and an aging Nazi who fought against them. Steiner also makes much of the symbolic identity between Jew and Nazi, going so far as to have one character speculate that Hitler himself was secretly Jewish and sought to kill his co-religionists simply to be "the final Adam. . . . What's the use of being a Jew, one of the chosen people, if there are millions of others? That's nothing to shout about. But to be the only one left. The last Jew. Kill all the others. And be the last" (98). That bizarre notion, which Steiner's critics greeted with particular scorn, is ultimately echoed in Hitler's final speech, when he claims Jewish precedents for his action if not quite Jewish ancestors. And yet thrillers almost always deal with multiple identities of this kind: perhaps the most commonplace trope in the genre is that Jew turns out to be former Nazi and Nazi turns out to be secret Jew. Once again, the point is that an idea which seems grotesque and offensive in a serious novel—Hitler as the Last of the Just—is acceptable in a spy thriller and might be equally acceptable in Steiner's *Portage* if that novel were seen *as* a spy thriller.

"I always wonder," Steiner told an interviewer, "about this enormous fascination of the intellectual for detective stories, espionage."[12] There would seem to be some possibility, then, that George Steiner the intellectual has himself been fascinated enough by spy thrillers to read some of them and to try his own hand at the genre in *The Portage to San Cristóbal* while simultaneously writing a serious novel about the Holocaust with the other hand. Many other contemporary writers have borrowed plot devices from a popular genre in order to put them to a serious purpose, as Steiner recently showed George Orwell doing in *1984 (New Yorker)*, but that would not seem to be quite accurate in this case. The mosaic-like structure and stereotypical characters of the spy thriller are not used by Steiner to lend anything in particular to the serious nature of Hitler's reappearance—if anything, they undermine seriousness by making Steiner's *Portage* all too similar to an entertainment like the one by

Len Deighton. Steiner's C.I.A. agent Marvin Crowbacker does not really comment upon American vulgarity any more sharply than Deighton's C.I.A. agent Melvin Kalkhoven, from whom he is virtually indistinguishable. Nor is Steiner attempting to use the serious theme of Hitler's capture to call into question the spy thriller genre by showing how inadequate that genre is to contain the unique horrors of Hitlerism. The theme of Nazi resurgence has been used by other spy thrillers in precisely the same way, and in *The Odessa File* by Frederick Forsyth, for one example, the cornered Nazi is also allowed to deliver an eloquent self-defense at the end. Steiner is neither borrowing from the spy thriller to serve the serious moral purpose of a Holocaust novel nor borrowing a theme from Holocaust literature to serve the thriller's ends of suspense and harmless excitement. He is rather combining two different genres to undermine *both,* to bring them into a diacritical collision with one another in order to demonstrate that language is equally inadequate at explaining the Holocaust and at trivializing it. "All my work arises out of thoughts on language" Steiner told an interviewer[13] and in a letter to Joseph Lowin Steiner made a remark even more to the point: "*The Portage* is 'about' the power of the word to 'un-create.' "[14]

If *The Portage* is read as thriller, the reader's reaction is a mixture of response to motifs familiar from other thrillers and dismay that the novel is reaching its conclusion too rapidly to combine these motifs in a satisfactory manner. The threads of the plot are never tied together; the novel stops before the confrontation which, in a well-constructed thriller, is the *raison d'être* of the entire book. The climactic speech by Hitler serves two functions at once: it not only denies the effort of Holocaust fiction to make sense of what occurred in history, it also denies the artificial unity imposed by a carefully orchestrated plot. Steiner's novel is made up of two different novels, combined for the most part by alternating a chapter of one with a chapter of the other. There are three specific links, however, between Hitler and his captors (the serious Holocaust novel), and the agents of all nations (the inhabitants of the highly stylized world of the spy thriller). First and foremost there is the shortwave radio, although it malfunctions and almost literally rots away. Yet at the end of chapter seven and the beginning of chapter eight, both sets of characters hear the same song on the radio, evidently in a language that none of them can understand. Then there is the Indian Teku, who has known the British agent in Orosso and later appears as a witness at Hitler's trial, even though he does not understand a word of what the old man says. Finally there are the helicopters, which conclude the novel with a noise that serves to drown out all language and suspend all understanding. Each of these three links is paralinguistic and shows the inability of the two genres to interact meaningfully with one another. Similarly, each of the two different genres within *The Portage* prevents the other one from reaching a satisfactory conclusion. The thriller is stopped cold by a speech about the Holocaust, which cannot be answered because the thriller's convergence plot makes any possible answer inaudible. Thus, each genre uncreates the other, and in each case the language that manipulates an audience is followed by the silence that is the only possible reply to linguistic manipulations.

While a reader who expects a serious novel about the Holocaust may well be offended by Steiner's conclusion, the reader who expects a spy thriller—and this expectation is encouraged as the novel proceeds—will probably be, if not equally offended, at least equally frustrated in these expectations. The reader who expects the two genres to be meaningfully combined, however, will experience a different sort of reaction, one that would undoubtedly please George Steiner. That reader would be left thinking not about the Holocaust but about the impossibility of writing any sort of fiction about a subject as overwhelming as the Holocaust; that reader would be left thinking not about the language of power, but about the powerlessness of language.

NOTES

[1] Len Deighton, *XPD* (New York: Knopf, 1981) 82. All page references to this edition are referred to by page number.

[2] Hyam Maccoby, "George Steiner's Hitler," *Encounter* 58, no. 5 (May 1982):30.

[3] George Steiner, *The Portage to San Cristóbal of A. H.* (New York: Simon and Schuster, 1982) 67.

[4] Melvin Plotinsky, "George Steiner: In Defense of Hitler," *Jewish Frontier* 50, no. 4, 18.

[5] Sigmund Freud, *Moses and Monotheism* (London: Hogarth Press, 1939) 164.

[6] Hugh Herbert, "Interview of George Steiner," *The Guardian,* 19 May 1981, 9.

[7] Joseph Lowin, "Steiner's Helicopters," *Jewish Book Annual* 41 (1983–1984): 55.

[8] Joseph Leonard, *New York Times,* 16 April 1982, 29.

[9] George Steiner, *Extraterritorial* (New York: Atheneum, 1967) 35.

[10] Bernard Berghonzi, "The Return of the Führer," *Times Literary Supplement,* 12 June 1981, 660.

[11] Alvin Rosenfeld, "Steiner's Hitler," *Salmagundi,* 52–53 (1981): 161.

[12] Mary Blume, "Interview with George Steiner," *International Herald Tribune,* 28–29 Nov. 1981, 14

[13] David Nathan, "Interview of George Steiner," *The Jewish Chronicle* (Mar. 26, 1982): 26.

[14] This letter, dated September 23, 1982, is in a file of invaluable material relating to Steiner's *Portage* that was kindly made available to me by Joseph Lowin.

3. WYNDHAM LEWIS'S *THE CHILDERMASS* (1928): THE SLAUGHTER OF THE INNOCENTS IN THE AGE OF CINEMA

Paul Tiessen

IN HIS MANY RESPONSES to twentieth-century culture, Wyndham Lewis (1882–1957) perhaps more than any other modern novelist or philosopher or critic persisted in making the cinema a complex metaphor for the "1984" which, he felt, had begun with the intensified media slaughter of the world's innocents—that is, of the helpless "gum-chewing World-pit" the media had created of massman everywhere—early in this century.[1, 2] Especially from the 1920s on, Lewis opposed the glorification of the global village (as Marshall McLuhan, Lewis's intellectual stepchild, was to call it, somewhat more euphorically than Lewis would have liked) created by the cinema and related technologies; he saw in the popular use of cinema the means and the metaphor for the debasement, devaluation, even dismemberment of the individual cultures of the world, in a world that through modern technologies had become "one big village."[3] In *The Childermass* (1928), a kind of mass for those whom the popular communications mechanisms had catapulted willy-nilly into the twentieth century, Lewis in various ways introduced film as an apocalyptic metaphor central to the meaning of his text.[4] Indeed, this novel—regarded often as his most difficult—can be read as a Lewis-guide on the place of film in modern society. With its absorption of narrative and descriptive images and techniques derived from Lewis's speculation about film, *The Childermass* is also one of those works which suggests that during the age of the silent movie, the "cinematic imagination" in Britain flourished more vigorously in literary—especially stream-of-consciousness fiction, which Lewis had rejected and was actually parodying, as he was film form, in *The Childermass*—than in film fiction.[5]

As Lewis scholars observe, *The Childermass* is a dramatization, a comic critique, as Robert Chapman says, of "the Bergsonian concept of la durée, [Samuel] Alexander's notion [in *Space, Time and Deity* (1920)] of 'Time as the soul of space,' and Whitehead's idea [in *Science and the Modern World* (1925)] of 'eternal objects' which 'haunt time like a spirit.'"[6] For all these, as also for fellow novelists such as James Joyce and Gertrude Stein, Lewis saw in the mechanics of cinema a correlative.[7] In particular, it was in the cinema's dependence on a mechanically driven shot-by-shot (even frame-by-frame) format[8] that Lewis found an important point of reference in delineating his sinister vision in *The Childermass*. Cinema represented for him other forms of discontinuity as well: an enforced rupture of the sense of sight—the specialized sense of the film audience—from the sense of touch; the intellectual disjunction, through the mechanical resuscitation of a space/time world captured and fixed on film, of a viewer's experience of the immediate and other levels of space/time; and, of course, through the deliberate or even unintentional uses of cinema, a political arbitrariness consequent upon the cinema's relentlessly imposed interpretations of past, present, or future events. In a simple but important way, Lewis's assessments of cinema as an instrument of fragmentation are succinctly summarized in *Snooty Baronet* (1932), where he mocked cinema's reliance on a rhetoric of discontinuity, on a mechanical imperative which forces viewers to gaze at actors on a screen who are "apt to *go out* at any moment, and turn up again, in some other place."[9] Modern forms of communication such as cinema, Lewis was suggesting, detach man from traditional forms of self-knowledge; they alter radically the coordinates of his space/time environment; they force upon him a bewildering restructuring of perception of human experience.

Around midcentury when Lewis, like George Orwell, identified historically a watershed in technological man's historical progress, he, unlike Orwell, looked back some decades and, rather dramatically, called the turning point "a New Year One."[10] He regarded the enduring effects of the destructive legacy of 1914–18 less as a function of the direct military violence of World War I than of the sudden ascendancy of media tyrannies which created the dystopia so dominated by cinema; it is at this historic moment—in the immediate aftermath of what we know as the years 1914–18 and of what Lewis called the Year One—that *The Childermass* actually takes place. The two protagonists of the novel represent less those young men who died in combat during the Great War than young men utterly disoriented by having been transported from a world of familiar to a world of recently invented media.

Like Orwell, Lewis observed often that control of new communications mechanisms gave the political elite the techniques they needed for the precise manipulation of the masses, but his emphasis was rarely on media content. (Indeed, in the end he put more emphasis on the nature of the mechanisms as tyrannies in their own right than on the question of the control of those mechanisms.) For example, in his philosophic treatise, *Time and Western Man* (1927) (itself in some ways a guide to *The Childermass)*, he expressed the concern that popular media more than military weaponry were likely to paralyze the modern world: "Democratic masses could be governed without a hitch by suggestion and hypnotism—Press, Wireless, Cinema. So what need is there . . . to slaughter them."[11] Again, in *Hitler* (1931), Lewis included what he called "film-plays" among the forms of governing by mass hypnotism, of "bringing about such a state of mind as is desired by the political interests financing those activities,"[12] such as the "Millionaire Film-mind" (304) he alludes to in *The Childermass*. Thus, even if a ruling party or class was not deliberately exploiting a medium such as film, Lewis was still pessimistic about the impact of such a medium, specifically about the consequences of a public vulgarized by its ubiquitous presence in the very world it was newly creating. In *The Doom of Youth* (1932), he distinguished between the awesome new power of popular media and the relative helplessness of the traditional centers of power in Washington or London:

> . . . whether openly or covertly, it is Press and
> Cinema hypnotism that rules Great Britain and
> America, not the *conversazione* at Westminster or the
> White House. But the spell-bound public, at the

27

hands of the popular press or by way of the film, has notions and beliefs pumped into it that are the *reverse* of any recognized tradition— whether in Religion, Law, Government, or Ethics . . . . [I]f I have an objection at all to these principles of indirect government in the democratic West, it is because, although revolutionary, it is purely destructive: and being "democratic" it is destructive of what the lowest average "low-brow" *Homme moyen sensuel* is disposed to hate and to destroy.[13]

The Childermass is Lewis's demonstration of government by cinema.

In *The Childermass* Lewis adapted for a literary form of discourse certain rules which, as he saw it, govern or typify modes of expression in film. By subjecting his protagonists (even, as we shall observe, his reader) to a kind of literal application of the mechanics of film form, by turning them into film spectators (and ultimately, as a consequence, into film characters), Lewis exposes the tendencies he saw as inherent in film technique. In a way, Lewis's is an ominous, apocalyptic treatment of the very tendencies Vertov at about the same time affectionately mocked and celebrated in his film, *The Man With the Movie Camera* (1929).

It is the observable physical characteristics of the physical environment of *The Childermass* that are stressed and, indeed, that are the main concern in the first half of the novel. This environment, bathed in an "apocalyptic coloration" (10), is a kind of surreal afterworld for the two protagonists, Pullman and Satterthwaite (or Pulley and Satters, as they are often called), who find themselves in it after their death in the familiar world, the "earlier dispensation" (166) of solid space and linear time. By applying quite literally the laws of cinema to subvert the conventions of literary narrative, Lewis was able to illustrate how a society could be technologically, ultimately politically, sabotaged.

For example, in the first sentence of *The Childermass* we read, "The city lies in a plain, ornamented with mountains" (1). As we continue to read, the awesome solidity of the third-person narrative—with its apparently authoritative, omniscient speaker who refers to the city, the plain, and the ring of mountains with objective surety—is steadily undermined. As Chapman summarizes, "Obser-

28

vable reality shifts perpetually; solid-state physics are constantly disintegrating; flux is embodied in the new ontology. Everything is in the state of becoming something other; nothing has stability or substance."[14] The text becomes a kind of sci-fi map, a figurative but graphic exegesis of life after Year One. By the time we come close to the end of the novel, we actually learn that the apparently solid parts of the landscape are really fictions—indeed, film-fictions, we might say—within the fiction, fictions quite artificially fabricated by the Bailiff, the administrator/tyrant who rules this new world. The mountains of the opening sentence, the reader finally discovers, are in fact "pukka mountains" (177), fake mountains of plaster or masonry. The ruler of this phantasmagoric, Bergsonian universe had this "landmark" (177), as he calls it, "fixed up" (177) himself, had it modeled after some mountains in Iceland. But it is a landmark which easily "goes out," like an image on a movie screen.[15] In *The Childermass*, a novel concerned with "accelerated media change as a kind of massacre of the innocents,"[16] Lewis includes the reader among the innocents.

When the reader meets Pulley and Satters, initiates in the "dead environment" (3), they are in a transit camp alongside a river which represents Bergson's durational flux, the stream-of-consciousness of Joyce, the mechanism of cinema. Here they await with other appellants the Bailiff's decision to admit them to the Heaven apparently represented by the city—the so-called Magnetic City—visible sometimes across the river. During their wanderings along the river, Pulley and Satters are confronted unexpectedly by what the reader may take as a version of a Lewisian movie scene:

> Satters in the dirty mirror of the fog sees a hundred images, in the aggregate, sometimes as few as twenty, it depends if his gaze is steadfast. Here and there their surfaces collapse altogether as his eyes fall upon them, the whole appearance vanishes, the man is gone. But as the pressure withdraws of the full-blown human glance the shadow reassembles, in the same stark posture, every way as before, at the same spot—obliquely he is able to observe it coming back jerkily into position. One figure is fainter than any of the rest, he is a thin and shabby mustard yellow, in colouring a flat daguerreotype or one of the person-

nel of a pre-war film, split, tarnished and transparent
from travel and barter. He comes and goes; sometimes he is there, then he flickers out. (14–15)

These beings or images which flood Satters' eye when it is only
passively gazing are called "peons" in the novel. They move jerkily
about like the apparently eyeless characters we sometimes see in
very old silent movies: "Grey-faced, . . . their eyes are blank,
like discoloured stones" (12). Their erratic rushing about reminds us
of the uncontrollable movements of the actual film actors Lewis described in *Filibusters in Barbary* (1932), a kind of travel book: "fifty
dumb characters in search of an author dumb enough to concoct a
plot and text for them . . . swarmed forward, vociferous and re-
plete with a strident quality that was so thin as to stamp them any-
where as screen-folk—creatures, that is, of an art one remove from
the shadow-picture."[17]
    Without recourse to other senses such as touch, or to prior ex-
perience, to intellect or memory, an amazed and curious Satters
stares at the peons: "The effort to understand is thrown upon the
large blue circular eyes entirely: but the blue disk is a simple regis-
ter. . . . What are these objects that have got in? signal the mus-
cles of the helpless eye: it distends in alarm; it is nothing but a
shocked astonished apparatus, asking itself if it has begun to work
improperly" (15). Unable to control his sense of balance under these
circumstances, Satters stumbles, falls to the ground, and brings
Pulley down with him. Finally, the scenes with the peons end, as
though with a fade-out—"In the course of a minute they have con-
vulsively faded" (18–19)—and Pulley and Satters, released from the
influence of this movie scene, regain their balance.
    But a little later, as they continue their walk along the river, yet
another episode occurs in terms which allude to film. As the distance
to the landmarks around them suddenly begins to vary, Pulley, who
arrived in this afterlife some time before Satters and who has adop-
ted some of the Bailiff's evasive explanations of the surroundings,
reveals himself to be something of an apologist for the film-reality
that is imposed on them:

> "What are those hills?"
> "Hills? Where? There are no hills. They're noth-
> ing!" Pullman crossly exclaims.

"I didn't know."

"Nothing at all, not hills."

The distance to the city varies; Satters repeatedly looks over, lunging his head to catch it at its changes and at last says:

"Doesn't that look smaller sometimes?"

"What?" Pullman looks round indignantly.

"Sometimes it looks smaller to me than others."

"Certainly not! Whatever makes you think!"

The whole city like a film-scene slides away perceptibly several inches to the rear as their eyes are fixed upon it.

"There!" exclaims Satters pointing.

"Oh that! I know, it looks like it. But it isn't so. It's only the atmosphere." (21–22)

Like before, the film-scene, flourishing in an atmosphere conducive to its dominant role, takes its toll of tactile correlatives; with his eyes fixed upon the city, Satters "trips repeatedly" (24).

Pulley has been in the Bailiff's realm long enough to have been subjugated by its spatial and temporal tentativeness, by its cinema-like qualities. When Satters catches a glimpse of him shortly after, at a point when Pulley seems to be particularly elusive and "immaterial" (26), what he sees is a kind of film close-up of his face: "he can catch sight of a large face manoeuvring. It is Pullman's head, very large" (27). A moment later, he sees Pulley as if in long shot: "Pullman is a long way off, a small shapely figure" (27). Pulley has become like one of the peons, one of Lewis's screen-folk. Indeed, when Satters looks again at Pulley's face, he "gazes into a sallow vacant mask, . . . till it is blank and elementary, in fact the face of a clay doll." Clapping his hands, he cries out, "Why, you are a peon!" (30).

Still later, the protagonists' arrival in a new setting suggests yet again the space/time disorientation typical for a Lewisian film-viewer. Indeed, when Pulley, in a later novel of the trilogy that begins with *The Childermass*, recalls the present occasion, he remembers his having gotten into "a scene of two hundred years ago —like turning a cinematograph backwards and holding it rigid."[18] In a statement recalling Lewis's own description elsewhere[19] of time-regions as mechanically fixed and even reversible, Pulley proclaims without any sign of Lewis's own regret: "Reversibility is the proof that the stage of perfection has been reached in machine construction—it's the same with us, in my opinion. Here we are going backwards aren't we?" (96). As the solidity of physical space breaks down, Pulley gushes: "It's most remarkable how two times can be made to fit into one space and that only a functional one; no one can call this physical except by courtesy or for convenience" (94).

When this time-scene, with its diminishing, camera-eye perspective ends "in a black flash" (103), Pulley and Satters are again "flung upon their faces" (103). Appropriately, the river, which they had been trying to find just prior to this space/time event, now appears before them as they pick themselves off the ground. The Bergsonian flux/stream provides continuity along the episodic route of their adventures. It is not long, to be sure, until Satters finally joins Pulley in obedient mimicry of film actions, after Pulley has cracked him once on the head. His reaction recalls the sense of precise comic timing in the early slapstick films:

> Satters as Keystone giant receives the crack exactly in the right spot, he sags forward in obedient overthrow, true to type—as though after a hundred rehearsals, true to a second—and crashes to earth as expected, rolling up a glazed eyeball galore, the correct classical Keystone corpse of Jack-the-Giantkiller comedy. Pullman gazes down through his glasses at the prostrate enemy while the camera could click out a hundred revolutions. (111)

Society's need for cultural and intellectual renewal within the context of its technological environment, Lewis was saying in *The Childermass* as elsewhere, is desperate. In *The Childermass* the mechanics of a kind of rebirth are pathetically simulated by the Bailiff, using means grotesquely suited to the shallowness of media-produced man, and so actual rebirth never occurs. In the world controlled by this Bergsonian show-man, the coming of a phoenix, traditionally a symbol of rebirth, is arranged as part of an impressive—however ludicrous—cinema spectacle. Pulley and Satters and the other appellants watch a kind of film-show which flashes on the other side of the river, where the walls of the Magnetic City are often seen. It is, think some of the appellants, a slick picture of Babylon five thousand years ago, not unlike, perhaps, the Babylon of Griffith's *Intolerance:* "Oh look!" shouts one of them, "That must be Babylon! I've seen it on the pictures" (137).

When one of the appellants dares to assert, "It's a cinematograph!" (139), the denial by another—"No, it's not a cinematograph" (139)—represents more a sly smirk than a denial by Lewis. Indeed, the narrator suggests that this "phantom picture" (137) is to be watched, like a movie, "upon the turning down of the lights" (137); and when the show is over the Bailiff admits: "They always do that film business when the Phoenix comes. It's quite pretty, but as archaeology it's all nonsense I'm afraid. I hope you enjoyed it?" (144).

When an eager member of the audience, still intellectually capable of admitting his confusion about the merging of physical and photographed reality, asks the Bailiff, "Please, sir, is it a real bird?," the Bailiff's reply only seems evasive: "No, not real but quite real enough" (144). In the mechanized world of cinema, surrogate forms of rebirth are all that can be attempted.

Mass-man, Lewis insisted, had become the uncritical heir to what he was invited to consider as the benefits of this century's media explosion. It was the modes of expression of those very media that Lewis, in works such as *The Childermass*, was able to employ "as a means of clairvoyance."[20]

NOTES

[1] In the present essay I make brief references especially to works Lewis wrote in the late 1920s and early 1930s, shortly before and after his publication of *The Childermass* in 1928: *Time and Western Man, Hitler, Snooty Baronet, Doom of Youth,* and *Filibusters in Barbary.* However, Lewis's uses of film as metaphor continued to the end of his career; my essay in the forthcoming first issue of *Canadian Film Studies* (proposed for 1984) is a general introductory survey of some such uses throughout Lewis's polemical and fictional works, from the 1920s to the 1950s.

[2] *Filibusters in Barbary* (London, 1932: New York: National Book Club, 1980) 104. Though Lewis repeatedly castigated the actual and symbolic roles of film in twentieth-century life, he did

here and there suggest his love of certain German, Russian, and French films, as well as those of Chaplin. However, he generally avoided references to specific films or directors and, too, attacked Chaplin's place in the popular mass-mind.

[3] *America and Cosmic Man* (New York: Doubleday, 1949) 21.

[4] The "Childermass" is the festival of the Holy Innocents, commemorating the slaughter of the children (see Matthew 2:16) by Herod. My references to Lewis's *The Childermass* (London: Methuen, 1928) will be noted in the text. Italics in any quoted excerpts are also in the original.

[5] Dorothy Richardson's *Pilgrimage,* the first installment of which appeared in 1915, is an early example of one of the best of the "cinematic" (to use the common metaphor) novels. See my articles on Richardson's fiction and her theory of film in *Literature/Film Quarterly,* III, 1 (Winter 1975) and in the 1983 *Proceedings of the Purdue University Seventh Annual Conference on Film* (West Lafayette, 1983). Lewis himself often attacked James Joyce and Gertrude Stein for what he regarded as their "cinematic" experiments in literary fiction.

[6] Chapman, *Wyndham Lewis: Fictions and Satires* (New York: Vision Press, 1973) 168.

[7] Joyce and Stein, of course, were "stream of consciousness" writers, writers championing the subjective, internal approach, writers whom Lewis criticized for having capitulated (to quote Jameson's succinct summary) to "the fetishization of temporality and the celebration of Bergsonian flux." See Frederic Jameson, *Fables of Aggression: Wyndham Lewis, The Modernist as Fascist* (Berkeley: University of California Press, 1979) 3.

[8] In my essay, "The Critic, the Film and the Astonished Eye" (in *Figures in a Ground: Canadian Essays on Modern Literature Collected in Honor of Sheila Watson,* eds. Diane Bessai and David Jackel [Saskatoon, 1978] 125–40), I draw attention to Lewis's emphasis on cinema as discontinuous and fragmented. The cinema's shot-by-shot shock tactics take advantage not only of the editing technique known as cutting, but also of the ever-shifting boundaries imposed by the frame (or screen). Both of these technological imperatives of the medium reinforce the tension and opposition between what is shown in the shot and what is held back permanently or temporarily.

⁹ *Snooty Baronet* (London: Haskell House, 1932) 163. Italics as in the original text. The actions of Michel-Ange, when he is at the movie theatre in Godard's *Les Carabiniers* (1963), illustrate Lewis's interpretation—though in a narrowly specific and absurdly comic way—of the effects of the film medium.

¹⁰ *Self Condemned* (Chicago: Univ. of Chicago Press, 1965 [1954]) 91.

¹¹ *Time and Western Man* (Boston: Beacon, 1957 [1927]) 137.

¹² *Hitler* (London: Haskell House, 1931) 136–37.

¹³ *Doom of Youth* (London: Haskell House, 1932) viii.

¹⁴ Chapman, 165.

¹⁵ In his 1980 essay, "A Reading of *The Childermass*," Alan Munton, commenting on the narrative reliability of the opening of the novel, suggests that "A concrete reality that seemed to be endorsed by the fiction-making activity itself turns out to be an invention in which the author allows us to believe only for as long as it suits purpose." See Munton's essay in *Wyndham Lewis: A Revaluation,* ed. Jeffrey Meyers (Montreal, 1980) 127. Munton does not mention cinema. Chapman, however, notes that the opening paragraphs of the novel function "like a long, panning camera shot." Pullman and Satters, the two antiheroes, remind him of "a Laurel and Hardy version of Don Quixote and Sancho Panza." See Chapman, 166 and 168.

¹⁶ McLuhan, *Understanding Media* (Toronto: Univ. of Toronto Press, 1968 [1964]) 31. McLuhan has said that "in *The Childermass* Lewis used the medium of the talking picture before it had been invented. It is a talkie in full colour." See McLuhan's essay, "Lewis's Prose Style," in *Wyndham Lewis: A Revaluation,* ed. Jeffrey Meyers (Montreal, 1980) 66. McLuhan's claims concerning talkies and colour are certainly more extravagant—though that is not the issue here—than any I make for Lewis in this essay. Actually, his claims are not strongly borne out by the novel; indeed, in the manner in which I suggest Lewis has used film here, it is largely the silent, pre-color cinema from which he has borrowed.

¹⁷ *Filibusters in Barbary,* 91.

¹⁸ *Monstre Gai* (London: Methuen, 1955) 219. *Monstre Gai* is Book Two of Lewis's trilogy, *The Human Age.* Book Three is *Malign Fiesta* (London, 1955).

¹⁹ *Time and Western Man,* 231.

²⁰ McLuhan, "Lewis's Prose Style," 67.

4. THE DISINTEGRATION AND RECONSTRUCTION OF ARTEMIO CRUZ

Harry Rosser

THE DEATH OF ARTEMIO CRUZ is a text which lends itself to objective analysis as well as reader-response approaches. Whether Carlos Fuentes's novel is autonomous and possesses determinate meaning or is best viewed as a springboard for the experience of subjective interaction is a concern that is subordinated to the process of giving meaning to a text that initially does not make sense.[1] Since it first appeared, a number of studies have formally established the system of relations according to which this literary work functions.[2] But Fuentes himself has questioned the possibility of a completely objective basis for the procedure of criticism. In fact, he requires the reader to break with traditional narrative expectations and develop a new set of reading conventions when approaching *The Death of Artemio Cruz*. As early as 1962, the year his controversial third novel was published, he stated: "I have an idea of the public in Mexico, but I want this public to think more, to participate more: not just to receive what I give them, but to have them as a co-participant, as a co-creator with me."[3] The text, in other words, has a transitive function acknowledged by its author, who seeks a literary response. Actually, he demands it.

Given this intention on Fuentes's part, the reader must resort to a kind of trial and error reading process. Juxtapositions and disjunctions that elude immediate comprehension abound in the novel.

There are details that contradict each other and narrative perspectives that interject themselves at random. The writer's creativity involves a willful act of apparent disintegration of coherences.[4] The reader has no alternative but to respond by engaging in the reconstruction of a new dimension of reality. The reader's task is partially abetted by the consciousness of the protagonist who must piece together his own life during the few hours left to him on his deathbed. Artemio Cruz undergoes the tortuous process so that he may liberate himself from the divisions between his past, present, and future. Fuentes's aesthetic consciousness obligates the reader to suffer and become enlightened through a parallel, although different, process of reconstruction. In effect, the reader must undergo a spiritual crisis that is similar to the one that Artemio Cruz, and, indeed, Mexico suffer.

The operations that lead from Fuentes's text to this particular understanding are grounded on the primary convention which Jonathan Culler calls "the rule of significance." The text is read "as expressing a significant attitude to some problem concerning man and/or his relation to the universe."[5] The experience of the text leads eventually to a coherence and significance that is convincing to the reader: he participates in both a biographical and a historical trajectory—the life of Artemio Cruz and of Mexico in the twentieth century. Fuentes prompts considerable thinking about what constitutes a nation and why. He portrays Mexico as being divided between the reality of the country (i.e., how it has developed and the situation in which it now finds itself) and men like Artemio Cruz, a symbol of what Mexico could have been, as well as how it was betrayed.

Fuentes's narrative kaleidoscope radiates from three fixed points: the first-person singular view, based on present consciousness; the third-person historical vantage point; and the curious second-person singular perspective of projection or preintention which relies on the future tense, often *after* the fact. A lack of chronology accentuates the multiplicity of the perspectives themselves, the events that are narrated, and the coincidental manifestation of alternative ways of thinking and behaving under specific circumstances.

Critics have been intent on pinning down the primary perspectives. Osorio refers to them as consciousness, memory, and the unconscious; Jara associates them with three separate narrators, arguing that the "You" form of address comes from a narrator who informs the protagonist of certain aspects of his "vital discourse" that are unknown to him.[6] For Sommers, the controversial second person future perspective functions as "a mysterious other voice, akin to Cruz's alter ego."[7]

Be that as it may, of more importance than classification is the fact that the reader is unequivocally drawn into the text by the two direct forms of address. The use of "I" and "You" puts the imagination into play in a most personal way. The "He" form pulls it toward an objective level of operation. The perspectives are juggled in such a way as to "actualize" or "realize" the text, as Wolfgang Iser puts it. The process is one in which there is a "convergence of reader and text."[8] Each reader fills in gaps or areas of indeterminacy in his own way.

The concept is applicable here as the reader goes about fulfilling what is already implicit in the structure of *The Death of Artemio Cruz.* According to Iser, a literary work has two poles, the artistic and the aesthetic: ". . .the artistic refers to the text created by the author, and the esthetic *[sic]* to the realization that the literary work cannot be completely identical with the text, or with the realization of the text, but in fact must lie halfway between the two."[9] This is a phenomenological theory of art which coincides remarkably with Fuentes's aforementioned view of the reader as a "co-creator" of the work who is called upon to supply unwritten portions of the text. In an effort to find the balance and unity of the work, the overall "picture" must be created from the *fabula,* or the reconstructed sequence of events in Artemio Cruz's life, and the *sjuzet,* or discourse, which is the particular order (in this case, disorder) in which the events are placed at the reader's disposal.[10]

An example of the way in which these narrative principles function in Fuentes's novel may be seen in the order of immediate events leading up to Cruz's marriage of convenience to the aristocratic Catalina Bernal. The reader must unscramble the events in order to make sense of what actually takes place at random intervals. Loveluck has drawn attention to the well-known film technique of temporal and spatial *montage* in which a barrage of images develops the object on a variety of levels.[11] In this particular situation, the approximately one dozen fragments that have to do with Cruz meeting Don Gamaliel and his daughter are presented in such a way that the actual visit to the mansion occurs well before Cruz has even set foot in the town where the Bernal family lives. The protagonist's discovery of Catalina's identity upon seeing her on the street is described after Cruz has already spent an entire evening over dinner with her and her father. Cruz's recollection of a comment made in town about how Don Gamaliel stole land from the Church flashes by before he has even entered the bar where he gleans that particular piece of information. This discourse keeps the reader in suspense and adds particular irony to the events whose causality is initially blurred.

And such is the procedure throughout the entire novel. The reader must actively look for links, trace origins, forecast consequences, discover consistency, arrange the material at hand, and interpret meaning on top of it all. Iser has pointed to the need to organize and reorganize the various data that a text offers. "These are the given factors," he says, "the fixed points on which we base our 'interpretation,' trying to fit them together in the way that we think the author meant them to be fitted."[12] By this, Iser underscores that the perception of a work of art involves an act of creation, for the constituents of the whole that is in form must be ordered.

The piecemeal plan of Fuentes's work is subtly signaled to the reader on the opening page:

> And now I am awake, but I don't want to open my eyes. Just the same, although it is not desired, something shimmers insistently near my face, something seen through closed eyes in a fugue of black lights and blue circles. I tighten the muscles of my face and open my right eye and see it reflected in the squares of silvered glass that encrust a woman's purse. I am this, this am I: old man with his face reflected in pieces by different-sized squares of glass . . . .[13]

The image of the fragmented mirror suggests a disintegration or dissolution of the self to both the protagonist and the reader. The "failure story" that Cruz and the reader will review at a limited number of critical junctures necessarily begins with the recognition of death as a form of liberation from a corrupt existence. Death to a former self, as in Cruz's case, represents a new course, the possibility of a different life. From the outset, it is implicit in the structure of the novel that the reader must follow a *via crucis* with Fuentes so that the dying Artemio Cruz may pass on and be free.

There is something that restrains the protagonist, however, that prevents his immediate demise. And that is the force of memory. Until he understands how he has gotten to the point where he now is, his life cannot end. The freedom that can come from the painful awareness of the immediacy of death can provide a new foundation for the reconstruction of the idealism that Cruz gave up in his youth. The reader pays a good deal of attention to the memory perspective as it becomes increasingly clear that the past is not as disturbing to Cruz as the present:

> What did I do yesterday? If I think about what I did yesterday, I'll stop thinking about what is happening now. That's a lucid thought. Very lucid: think yesterday. You're not so crazy, you don't suffer so much, you can think yesterday, yesterday, yesterday. (7)

The present is, in part, the memory of what could have been. There is a definite division between Cruz's past and his present: Cruz the youth and Cruz the adult are two unrelated people. Cruz does not have a clear awareness that there is such a split, however. He is confused and struggles with the concept, but in so doing he is able to recall the past and dredge up what he once was:

> Artemio Cruz is sick, he does not live. No, he lives! Artemio Cruz did live once. He lived several years. Years, not yearns. No, he lived several days. Days, not daze. His twin, Artemio Cruz, his double. Yesterday Artemio Cruz, he who lived only a few days before dying, yesterday Artemio Cruz, who is . . . I am I, and he, I, is another . . . yesterday. (7)

The third person singular comes forcefully into play to indicate that the division does exist within Cruz even though he is unable to relate to it at first. If he could clearly understand, then the first person would speak. Through these devices of shifting perspectives, Fuentes focuses on the need for unity within oneself before attempting a new beginning. This will only happen for Cruz at the exact moment in which he becomes aware of how he has reached that particular point. When he realizes why he made certain critical decisions, he will no longer fear his past and his memory of it. He must grapple with what it is that condemns him, and so does the reader. When the recollection of what the protagonist *could* have been becomes what *may* (in good faith) be, then Cruz will be able to die in peace.

The narrative discourse on the life of Artemio Cruz consists of a series of crucial alternatives: honesty versus ambition, responsibility versus profit, career versus conscience. They form not only the trajectory of his existence but the very destiny that he and the reader must reconstruct. It is these same alternatives, moreover, that fragment his identity and his understanding of himself. In the text, the self is broken down into its constituent elements, no longer functioning as the main source of meaning. In order to regain a sense of self as a given that is not totally dependent on how it interacts with others for its definition, the "I" of Artemio Cruz must be reestablished.

In the beginning, Cruz was a revolutionary but he betrayed the movement in an effort to preserve the love that he shared with Regina, the only person in his life with whom he is able to be complete. The terrible irony is that he forsakes his own positive values in an effort to be united with the object of his love—and then she dies. Cruz maneuvers himself into powerful positions among the alienated elite who claim to lead the country. The leadership they offer is devoid of the reform-mindedness that Cruz had once advocated. He turns his back on himself and on his country because it is too difficult to maintain a set of ideals when one is not whole.

When Cruz loses Regina he also loses all sense of unity, of integrity, and gives himself over completely to a life of corruption and self-aggrandizement. He judges his success by superficial standards in a headlong pursuit of materialism in which things come to replace sentiment and feeling. Eventually Cruz recognizes a gradual separation between his true desires and the material objects that he pursues, but the pattern of substitution itself is one of the great mistakes that he allows to characterize his existence.

Another major turning point for Cruz occurs when he succeeds in bribing his way out of jail but decides to leave behind his future brother-in-law, Gonzalo. Cruz chooses to follow a course that is different from that of his idealistic cell-mate. This particular decision is of utmost importance for it reflects the deliberate abandonment of the ideals for which Cruz had presumably been fighting. Gonzalo is the only person that Cruz will ever meet who truly embodies the spirit of the Revolution at its best. The movement fails in many respects, and Gonzalo dies; but at least he dies with a clear sense of how and why the Revolution faltered.

Gonzalo understands the development of the Revolution like no other character in the novel. At first he denies the importance of leaders for the success of the movement, but he comes to realize that it is they who ended up betraying it:

> So that's the irony. They are the only choices possible. I don't know whether you remember the beginning. It was a short time ago, but it seems so far away now. Leaders didn't matter then. It wasn't a war to raise up a *caudillo,* but to raise up all men.
> (185)

It is through Gonzalo, then, that the reader learns how the Revolution was untracked by people of limited vision who turned their back on the movement and formed factions.

The division between Gonzalo's goals and hopes for the Revolution and Cruz's abandonment of any such revolutionary aspirations is something that Gonzalo understands, but not Cruz. By deciding to leave Gonzalo, Cruz communicates his own inability to confront the significance of the alternatives: he can remain with Gonzalo, nurturing the few ideals that he has left, and die, or he can desert Gonzalo and what he, Cruz, could have been, and choose a new course to follow.

But Cruz operates as though the first choice did not exist, denying the difference between the two courses of action. Nevertheless, he is not able to escape his destiny, nor his memory. Gonzalo's ideals do not die when he dies, for Artemio Cruz carries them in his memory, at least, and later passes them on—almost inadvertently—to his own son, Lorenzo.

Cruz constantly lives with the past in the form of Catalina. The sister of Gonzalo is well-aware of her husband's shortcomings, of his evil side, but she does not know the real circumstances of her brother Gonzalo's death. Having married Cruz by arrangement between her father and him, she spends her energy defending her family's honor against a man she does not like. She bitterly refuses to give in to her husband, on any level:

> I have to make my mind up. I have no other choice
> than to be this man's wife until I die. Why not accept
> it? Yes: easy to think, hard to do. It is not so easy to
> forget why I hate him. God. God, tell me if I myself
> am destroying my chance for happiness. Tell me if I
> ought to put him above my duty as a sister and a
> daughter. . . . (100–101)

Catalina never allows Cruz to forget how her brother and son died. He feels constantly watched by a woman bent on calling attention to his acts of treachery. The conflicts within him are reflected in the conflicts between him and Catalina. She is a relentless reminder of the martyred Gonzalo, of an unfinished revolution, and of their betrayal by corrupt men like her husband.

Catalina serves as a reminder to Cruz in another important way as well. He knows that he cannot ever recapture the same kind of love he felt for Regina. Regina, who represents his innocent past, his idealism, and his capacity for true love, no longer exists. Cruz's wife accentuates his awareness that he is not the same person that he once was and Cruz feels the weight of his wrong decisions, of his age, and of his internal dissolution. Catalina keeps him ever mindful of their son who died fighting for the Republican cause in the Spanish Civil War. Ironically, Lorenzo believed in the ideals that his father held fleetingly as a young man. Before dying, Lorenzo writes:

> You would do the same Papá. You didn't stay out of
> it at home. What do I believe? I don't know. You
> brought me here. You taught me this life. . . . It
> has been as though you were living your life over
> again. Do you understand? (219)

Whatever the explanation, Catalina remains inflexible in her belief that Cruz is solely to blame for the death of their son. When he looks at his wife, Cruz can see that she does not understand; but he recognizes that the memory of Lorenzo is a reminder of what he himself could have been, of what he is not. Cruz faces his past and finally discovers that there is something in him of his past that still lives, and it is this positive element that was inherited by his son. Cruz's past finally comes to be a part of his present.

In the process of understanding who he really is from his own son, Cruz has completed the trajectory of his destiny. He begins as a youth—idealistic, innocent, revolutionary. He loses his love and his idealism; he loses himself, becoming a fragmented being, a man with many parts but no nexus. Once he leaves his birthplace, he fights against looking back because to do so would remind him of what could have been. But his destiny finds him in the future. When he reaches his last moments on earth, when he has reached the future toward which he had been looking since his youth, he realizes that the future is only a moment in the present of destiny.

Just before it is too late, Cruz discovers that he cannot escape his destiny, that he has to choose among alternatives and give assent to the consequences of deliberate decision. Once he accepts the divisions within him he is able to become complete, unified. And it is at this precise moment in his existence that he is able to return to his youth. He recognizes what he has come to be and how he has used his power, knowing in his final moments that within him lives the young man with the seed of lasting idealism. He understands that only in the reconstruction of his memory does he live:

> Time that, once it loses the opportunity to live, is forever wasted. Time that is incarnate in the unique being called you, now a boy, now a dying old man, a being who in a mysterious ceremony links together tonight, the little insects glowing against the dark cliff, and the immense stars whirling in silence against the infinite backdrop of space. (302)

The moment that he is able to return to his past, memory becomes a satisfied desire through which Cruz is now permitted to see his ideals. When he is fully able to remember, he understands who he is and becomes one within himself. When he is complete, a whole man, he is able to die: he is able to recognize the birth of a new way of life for a satisfied man, for a free man. By the end of his life — and of the novel, which includes a description of his birth, Cruz has completed the trajectory of his destiny: a circle.

In this absorbing and self-reflexive literary work, the life of Artemio Cruz and the history of Mexico are inextricably bound up by writer and reader who join together in an interpretive act. The resolution that Cruz makes, Mexico must also make. Through the trajectory of the protagonist's life, Fuentes offers a message regarding the future of his country. The writer begins his novel with the most recent stage of Cruz's life, making it implicit that so begins the recent history of Mexico—with corruption, factions, and internal power struggles rather than true concern for its people. Cruz is portrayed as an example of the kind of powerful men that betrayed the Revolution of 1910, of a leader whose concerns became separate from those of the majority of his countrymen. Just as the reader must reconstruct the life of Artemio Cruz, so must the history of Mexico be reconstructed in order to discover when, where, and why the Revolution failed. The vantage point must be that of the past as well as of the present in order to know how to establish a new course of thought and action. This requires a subjective process on Cruz's part, as well as that of the reader.

Just as the reader is called upon to participate directly in the disintegration, reconstruction, and interpretation of Fuentes's novel, so must there be active participation in the formation of a new Mexico in the latter stage of the twentieth century. Mexico presently suffers from a spiritual crisis much like that of Artemio Cruz, Fuentes implies. There is a lack of national idealism, lack of values that were lost with the gradual betrayal of the Revolution. The Revolution began with a kind of political innocence displayed on the part of people like the young Cruz in the midst of disruption and confusion. The identity conflict persists as the country continues to establish itself in the world picture.

In *The Death of Artemio Cruz* the protagonist symbolizes the potential and the possibility of restoring wholeness to a troubled nation—even in the eleventh hour. His son Lorenzo represents the continuation of the ideals of Cruz's youth. With these values, and the ability of a strong people to place themselves in their own history, by means of collective memory, a more unified, cohesive society can emerge. Such a society can more readily respond in a representative fashion to the needs of its people, fostering their spiritual as well as their material well-being.

Such is the nature and significance of a fragmentary and often complex literary work that engages the reader in the active process of making sense out of the text. Description of objective structures, formalization of sets of facts, assignment of functions to various elements of Fuentes's novel unquestionably have their value. But of principal significance is understanding *The Death of Artemio Cruz*

45

by establishing a limited number of connections and associations which create a meaningful view of human experience.

NOTES

[1] As Jane Tompkins soundly argues, "Although New Critics and reader-oriented critics do not locate meaning in the same place, both schools assume that to specify meaning is criticism's ultimate goal. This assumption not only joins these polemically opposed movements, it binds them together in opposition to a long history of critical thought in which the specification of meaning is not a central concern." "The Reader in History: The Changing Shape of Literary Response," in *Reader-Response Criticism: From Formalism to Post-Structuralism,* ed. Jane P. Tompkins (Baltimore: Johns Hopkins University Press, 1980) 201.

[2] See René Jara C., "El mito y la nueva novela hispanoamericana: A propósito de *La muerte de Artemio Cruz*"; Juan Loveluck, "Intención y forma en *La muerte de Artemio Cruz*," in *Homenaje a Carlos Fuentes,* ed. Helmy F. Giacoman (New York: Las Américas Publishing Co., Inc., 1971).

[3] Carlos Fuentes in Lee Baxandall, "An Interview with Carlos Fuentes," *Studies On The Left,* III (1962) 50.

[4] For an eloquent discussion of artistic endeavors as symptoms of our present human condition and the directions they are taking, see Erich Kahler, *The Disintegration of Form in the Arts* (New York: George Braziller, Inc., 1968).

[5] Jonathan Culler, *Structuralist Poetics* (Ithaca, N.Y.: Cornell University Press, 1976) 115.

[6] See Osorio and Jara articles in *Homenaje a Carlos Fuentes.*

[7] Joseph Sommers, *After the Storm: Landmarks of the Modern Mexican Novel* (Albuquerque: University of New Mexico Press, 1968) 155.

[8] Wolfgang Iser, *The Implied Reader: Patterns in Communications in Prose Fiction from Bunyan to Beckett* (Baltimore: Johns Hopkins University Press, 1974) 274.

[9] Iser, *The Implied Reader,* goes on to discuss the omissions that give a story its dynamism: "These gaps have a different effect on the process of anticipation and retrospection, and thus on the

'Gestalt' of the virtual dimension, for they may be filled in different ways. For this reason, one text is potentially capable of several different realizations, and no reading can ever exhaust the full potential, for each individual reader will fill in the gaps in his own way, thereby excluding the various other possibilities; as he reads, he will make his own decision as to how the gap is to be filled. In this very act the dynamics of reading are revealed" (279).

[10] These two principles of narrative are discussed at length by Jonathan Culler in Ch. 9, "Story and Discourse in the Analysis of Narrative" in *The Pursuit of Signs* (Ithaca, New York: Cornell University Press, 1981).

[11] Loveluck in *Homenaje a Carlos Fuentes*, 220–23.

[12] Iser, *The Implied Reader,* 285.

[13] Carlos Fuentes, *The Death of Artemio Cruz,* trans. Sam Hileman (New York: Farrar, Strauss and Giroux, 1964). All page references are to this edition.

5. WAR AND PASTORAL: THE TREATMENT OF LANDSCAPE AND VALUE IN KUROSAWA'S *KAGEMUSHA*

John Gourlie

IN THINKING OF Kurosawa's films, one can see that he makes distinctive use of the landscape. *Rashomon, The Seven Samurai,* and *Dersu Uzala* come readily to mind. Here and in his other films, the setting is handled to create images that strike us as utterly realistic, as impeccable in both gritty detail and striking vista. One has only to recall the gate and forest of *Rashomon;* the farmers' village, the outlaws' hideout, the forests and fields of *The Seven Samurai;* the immense Russian wilderness—be it mountain or steppe—that the army Captain and the old hunter trek through in *Dersu Uzala.* Certainly, *Kagemusha* stands in the distinguished tradition of these films, and Kurosawa uses his landscape with masterful skill to root the dramatic action in a setting that is at once visually arresting and absolutely convincing in its reality. In doing so, Kurosawa makes visible the interplay of dramatic values. Even more, he creates lasting images, images of overriding power, beauty, and significance.

In *Kagemusha,* Kurosawa handles his landscape so that it assumes dramatic value in several ways. Initially, the landscape assumes such value in a quite literal way. Although the clan Kurosawa depicts is at first besieging a rival clan's castle, that clan must retreat to the safety of its own mountain stronghold upon the death of its leader. Thus the landscape is literally the source of secure existence

48

for the clan. Later, a more figurative relationship between the clan and the landscape is achieved as the chief warriors and, by extension, their battalions, are identified symbolically with natural elements: mountain, fire, wind, and trees. Kurosawa works this out as the troops assemble under their symbolic banners and each general is identified in particular with one of the natural elements. The warlord himself is identified with the mountain: the symbolic significance is that, like a mountain, he is immovable in battle. Through such connections, the landscape—particularly the home territory of the clan—may be seen as the source of heroic samurai values, both preserving them and nurturing them.

Yet what seems especially noteworthy in *Kagemusha* is the manner in which Kurosawa uses the landscape to structure the action. To take a major example, Kurosawa's handling of water contributes significantly to the film's action. In the early part of *Kagemusha,* for instance, the forces besieging the castle cut off its water supply. In itself, this seems merely a sensible maneuver in siege tactics, but the train of events it sets in motion produces a major turn in the action. The warlord conducting the siege, Lord Takeda, wishes to hear the opposing lord play the flute that evening, as is his custom, to see if the lack of water has parched his throat. During the evening recital, Lord Takeda is shot by an enemy sharpshooter, a wound that ultimately leads to his death. Perhaps ironically, given this chain of events, Lord Takeda is secretly laid to rest at the bottom of his native lake, a few loyal confidants sailing through the mists and darkness to dispose of a large urn containing his remains.

Water returns in key scenes, and what is of interest is how Kurosawa develops the water imagery into a pattern of great significance. But unlike the symbolic identification of chief warriors with elements of nature, the pattern of water images is not readily apparent, and the scope of its importance becomes clear only in the last sequence of the film. Kurosawa advances the pattern further in one of the most riveting of all the episodes in *Kagemusha,* the scene wherein the ghost of the dead Lord Takeda appears to his stand-in during a nightmare. The nightmare constitutes a short Noh drama within the larger realistic drama of the film as a whole. The scene is enacted on a surreal landscape, a lake shore or beach. The thief, impersonating the dead warlord, is chased by the lord's ghost into the water. In overall effect, the scene conveys the nightmarish weight of responsibility for the clan's safety now fallen on the thief's shoulders. The vision is also prophetic. The lord's ghost warns against aggressive ventures outside their territory, setting a specific body of water as the boundary not to be crossed. The landscape—transfigured during the Noh drama of nightmare—thus seems to assume the transcendent values embodied in the dead leader and to link these values significantly with water.

Kurosawa extends the water imagery in scenes that resonate with these earlier scenes. The impostor leader is discovered and cast out of the royal compound. The actual expulsion occurs—as do other scenes of deep import in Kurosawa's work—during a heavy downpour. Soon thereafter, having chosen a new leader burning to do battle with clan enemies, the advisory council meets to decide the issue of war or peace. The meeting takes place aboard a ship afloat on the lake—this scene evoking the earlier burial scene in which the dead lord was laid to rest in the same lake from a similar if not identical boat. Having decided to go to war, the new leader marches his army out along the lake or river that forms the boundary the dead warlord warned them not to cross. As the army is about to cross the boundary, colors appear in the sky—a rainbow or aurora effect. Some samurai interpret the colors as the symbolic warning of the dead warlord not to proceed. Indeed, the pastel colors recall the much more lurid colors of the nightmare landscape in which the ghost uttered its prophecy.

Before discussing the final sequence wherein the water imagery assumes its full significance, I would like to delineate two or three other structural patterns that emerge from Kurosawa's handling of the landscape and culminate in the final scenes of *Kagemusha*. One such pattern alternates the natural outside landscape of mountains, lakes, and forests with the man-made interior settings of the castle and royal compound. *Kagemusha* opens with an interview between Lord Takeda and the thief look-alike in one of the rooms of the royal compound. Later, the action progresses to the fields outside the besieged castle, where Lord Takeda is soon felled by a bullet fired from its walls. This alternation between "inside" and "outside" suggests several things, but chief among them is that the strategies and policies arrived at "inside" are played out in broad actions "outside."

Kurosawa sustains this pattern in a more complex way when the thief assumes the role of Lord Takeda. The thief triumphs in a series of domestic encounters, all of which occur within the assembly hall of the royal compound. In turn, he convinces the loyal retainers, the wives, and the child that he is Lord Takeda. Then, on the battlefield, the thief leads the army to victory against the counterattack of the enemy, and his own troops finally sack the castle they were originally besieging. It is as though the thief's successful imitation of Lord Takeda on the domestic scene allows the cautious military policies of Lord Takeda to prevail on the battlefield.

Kurosawa uses the same pattern to establish the contrast after the thief has been ousted. Aboard ship, the succeeding ruler and his council decide to go to war, a scene enacted inside the ship's cabin. Later, the consequences of that decision are fatally played out on the battlefield in the concluding scenes of the film. While effective in its own right, this pattern of internal scenes of decision and external scenes of action also dovetails with several other landscape patterns.

Perhaps the most intricate of these patterns emerges from Kurosawa's use of walls. Initially the thief is arrested for prowling around the walls of the royal compound, and soon thereafter Lord Takeda is shot from the walls of the enemy castle. In the middle of the film, the thief is protected by a human wall of his own soldiers during battle, but after his disguise is penetrated, the thief is once more cast outside the walls of the compound. Among the most poignant of all the film's scenes are the shots of the thief as he looks wretchedly back through the open latticework of the fence that is now separating him from the boy—and the life—he has come to love. Finally, at the film's end, the thief is shot from the walls of the enemy barricade. The thief's death thus echoes Lord Takeda's death.

The last landscape pattern I would like to examine contrasts the mountains with the open plains. With the exception of the final battle, the battles that occur in *Kagemusha* take place in generally mountainous terrain. The mountain landscape is of special significance because the symbol for Lord Takeda is "mountain." The role of Lord Takeda during battle is to remain seated, figuratively immovable as a mountain and thus an inspiration to his troops. So it is meaningful that Lord Takeda dies—or at least that his death is discovered—when the bearers of his carriage rest atop one of the high ridges defending the clan's territory. It is meaningful, too, that the thief's successor leads the army out of the mountains for the doomed final encounter. Visually, Kurosawa underscores the importance of this foray by a change of landscape, for the final battle

51

occurs on the open plains. The contrast between the secure safety of the mountains and the mortal danger of the plains is absolute.

If, in part, the visual power of the last scene derives from the change in landscape—the change from mountain to plain—it derives in an equal, but more subtle, measure from the convergence in the scene of the various structural patterns as well—the patterns formed by Kurosawa's handling of water, of walls, and of interior decisions played out in exterior actions. But in the final analysis, it is Kurosawa's genius that gives us imagery of a power surpassing our ability to account fully for it. Here we become more deeply aware that Kurosawa is a master and that *Kagemusha* is a work of art. Here, too, we realize not only that the landscape is a major element in such imagery, but that the imagery is itself the riveting embodiment of idea, emotion, and value. And as in a painting, a poem, or a novel, it is such imagery that lives on in our imagination transmitting from generation to generation our most profound sense of what it is to be human.

Throughout *Kagemusha,* Kurosawa presents images that, in their collective force, are worthy of standing in the company of those Homer presents in *The Iliad.* But nowhere is the epic sweep or personal poignancy of the imagery more stunning than in the conclusion of the film. Like Homer, Kurosawa draws *Kagemusha* from history. The final battle is based on the Battle of Nagashino fought in 1575 between the forces of Takeda and Oda Nobunaga.[1] Kurosawa depicts events with historical accuracy, for Takeda's men in fact stormed across the Taki River toward wooden barricades from which Nobunaga's men, armed with matchlock rifles, mowed them down. But what is impressive is Kurosawa's transformation of historical fact into dramatic action and cinematic image.

In the final scenes, the action possesses a raw immediacy, and at the same time, the images conveying it have a great beauty. Kurosawa shows us the slaughter in the vivid agony of men and horses fallen upon the plain. Especially we see the animal anguish, intensified by slow motion and silence on the sound track, as the wounded horses struggle to rise. In the aftermath of such mass destruction, the thief, having come to identify his fate with that of the Takeda clan, chooses death with those men his "leadership" failed to save rather than a lone survival. He rises from the river weeds where he has been hiding, a horrified witness to the slaughter, and charges alone across the field of battle seeking to join those fallen in death.

As moving as these scenes are, Kurosawa elevates the battlefield carnage to tragedy in his closing images. From overhead, we see a lone samurai and the clan banner submerged in the river that swiftly bears them away. It is an image of supreme beauty. Somehow, in the mysterious flow of art—in the cinematic interweaving of sequence with sequence—an image thrusts to the surface that transcends its own genesis in realistic detail. Such is the image of the banner and warrior swept away by the river. For it suggests in the death of one the fate of all, in the lost battle the vanity of all human plans and actions, in the flowing river the sweeping forces of time and destiny that submerge all human existence and swiftly bear it into the undifferentiated wash of the eternal seas.

If we wish to contemplate an apocalyptic landscape, *Kagemusha* provides us with such a landscape without ever violating its natural realities. If "apocalypse" means revelation, *Kagemusha's* concluding image reveals at once the fate of man and the power of art to give it voice. And, as the master image-maker, Kurosawa deserves that silent awe, that homage one pays to the holy man or the sacred artist by whose imagery we catch a glimpse of human life in thrall to final things.

NOTE

1 See Noel Perrin, *Giving up the Gun: Japan's Reversion to the Sword, 1543–1879* (Boulder, Colorado: Shambhala Publications, 1980) 16–23; The Battle of Nagashino is also recounted in A. L. Sadler, *The Maker of Modern Japan: The Life of Tokugawa Ieyasu* (London: G. Allen and Unwin, 1937) 100–05; S. R. Turnball, *The Samurai: A Military History* (New York: Macmillan, 1977) 156–160; Michael Gibson, *The Samurai of Japan* (London: Wayland, 1973) 53; and George B. Sansom, *A History of Japan, 1334–1615* (Stanford: Stanford University Press, 1958–1963) 287–88. See also Perrin's note 44 on page 98.

6. KINDLY CONGRUITY: UTOPIAN AND DYSTOPIAN ELEMENTS IN HARDY'S LIFE AND WORKS

Fran E. Chalfont

ONE OF THE MOST valuable insights produced by recent Hardy scholarship is the reevaluation of his legendary pessimism and gloom. Thorough study of the opinions expressed in his published writings, letters, and conversations indicates that although his views were at times influenced by current personal or social crises and always reflected his awareness of nature's indifference to man, Hardy's overall outlook was not as negative as earlier critics had asserted. As the following two quotations reveal, "sympathetic realist" is a more precise description of Hardy's stance. In a 1904 conversation with critic William Archer he stated, ". . . my pessimism, if pessimism it be, does not involve the assumption that the world is going to the dogs. . . . On the contrary, my practical philosophy is distinctly meliorist. What are my books but one long plea against 'man's inhumanity to man'—to woman—and to the lower animals? Whatever may be the inherent good or evil of life, it is certain that men make it much worse than it need be." At home, Hardy had the following quotation from John Galsworthy affixed to the front of that author's photograph, "The optimist appears to be one who cannot bear the world as it is, and is forced by his nature to picture it as it ought to be; and the pessimist one who can not only bear the world as it is, but loves it well enough to draw it faithfully."[1] Taken as a whole, Hardy's works and life reveal the extremes of both visions: utopian and dystopian. Common to both is the importance of man as the dominant force in the creation of either environment.

Hardy was not impressed by conventional beauty spots or by the lure of the unexpected, valuing much more highly landscapes which in some way reflected human experience, "An object or mark raised or made by man on a scene is worth ten times any such formed by unconscious Nature. . . .The beauty of association is entirely superior to the beauty of aspect, and a beloved relative's old tankard to the finest Greek vase."[2] With respect to Hardy's life, the experiences of his boyhood years and the landscapes associated with them are now viewed as of primal importance in shaping his artistic vision and, consequently, his personal and creative utopias.

As Desmond Hawkins asserted in *Thomas Hardy's Wessex* (1983), the locale "which most dynamically vitalized Hardy's imagination" was his wooded home parish of Higher Bockhampton, which to the south bordered a fertile dairying region and to the east an arid stretch of scrub and sandy heathland.[3] Of all of Hardy's childhood memories, the one which he later artistically employed in several different forms is also the most "utopian" in its attempt to freeze the process of maturation and hold on to a moment perfect in its freedom from care and responsibility. This experience, as recalled in his autobiography, occurred while "he was lying on his back in the sun, thinking how useless he was, and covered his face with a straw hat. The sun's rays streamed through the interstices of the straw, the lining having disappeared. Reflecting on his experiences of the world as far as he had got, he came to the conclusion that he did not wish to grow up." It seemed enough "to remain in the same spot and to know no more people than he already knew (about half a dozen)" (*Life,* 15–16).

Nearly fifty years later, near the start of *Jude the Obscure,* Hardy used exactly the same experience in presenting the plight of his protagonist as he discovered that "Growing up brought responsibilities. . . . Nature's logic was too horrid for him to care for."[4] Finally, Hawkins equated the straw-hat episode, which for Hardy "stood out more distinctly" than any other during his first eight years with the situation in Hardy's poem, "Childhood Among the Ferns." Here, a small boy is playing amidst the luxuriant undergrowth on the heath near his home. By midsummer, these ferns can reach heights of four to five feet, thus making it easy for a child to sit beneath the fronds in a nest safe not only from rain, but also from change:

> The sun then burst and brought forth a sweet breath
> From the limp ferns as they dried underneath:
> I said, "I could live on here thus till death;"
> And queried in the green rays as I sate:
> "Why should I have to grow to man's estate,
> And this far-noised World perambulate?"[5]

Hawkins declared that the prominence of this experience in Hardy's memory and writings clearly reflected "his deep-rootedness in the world of his childhood, to the extent that the heath becomes his personal Eden. . . . [It] symbolized the aboriginal background connection, the taproot into the distant past, which was to be such a source of strength in Hardy's writing" (29, 31). In Hardy's works, however, the urge to stop the clock remains associated with childhood, a time which characters like Tess and Jude have too little of and can never recapture.

In *The Return of the Native,* Hardy's childhood Eden becomes Egdon Heath, the novel's only setting, which is endowed with an individuality which turns it into a practical Utopia for those in harmony with its spirit. Hardy's descriptions of Egdon reflect his intimacy with this locale and his assertion that beauty is derived from association and interfusion with human emotions. Far removed from traditional exemplars of landscape beauty, the heath is introduced as "a vast tract of unenclosed wild," which in a November twilight "embrowned itself moment by moment." It has no brightness of color, being comprised of "darkest vegetation" in total harmony with the darkening sky: "The somber stretch of rounds and hollows seemed to rise and meet the evening gloom in pure sympathy, the heath exhaling darkness as rapidly as the heavens precipitated it."[6]

The seeming gloom of this picture is soon countered by Hardy's assertion that for some persons "It was a spot which returned upon the memory of those who loved it with an aspect of peculiar and kindly congruity. . . .Twilight combined with the scenery of Egdon to evolve a thing majestic without severity, impressive without showiness, emphatic in its admonitions, and grave in its simplicity" (12). For Hardy, its appeal embodied a new concept of beauty, far different from orthodox stress upon charm and pleasantness of aspect. He argued that Egdon radiated "a chastened sublimity" much more in accord with the somberness which he believed would be the future dominant mood of man. Hardy saw Egdon as clearly reflecting the temperament of man while remaining impervious to external signs of human control. "It was at present a place perfectly accordant with man's nature—neither ghastly, hateful, nor ugly; neither commonplace, unmeaning, nor tame; but, like man, slighted and enduring; and withal singularly colossal and mysterious in its swarthy monotony" (13). For Hardy, then, this most familiar landscape embodied philosophic truths and a physical appeal no less important than those suggested to Wordsworth while viewing the countryside near Tintern Abbey.

In the novel, for those like the rustic natives who make no demands upon it, and for those like Clym Yeobright who consciously understand and love it, the heath returns security and fulfillment. While it offers a far from idyllic existence in materialistic terms, the heath provides a stable environment conducive to long-term contentment, perhaps as much as modern man can demand—or deserves.

Hardy's most conventional—and transient—utopia is depicted in *Tess of the d'Urbervilles*. Few will dispute the very special status that the title figure had for her creator. She was, argued Hardy, based upon a real person, and he spoke of her as such while defending his heroine during the first turbulent months after the novel's publication. Many years later, when in his eighties, Hardy developed a potentially embarrassing infatuation with Gertrude Bugler, the young actress who played Tess in a local dramatic version. For Hardy, his Tess was alive again, and the Bugler/Tess identification became more credible when it was later revealed that the actress' mother had, like Tess, also worked as a dairymaid not far from Hardy's childhood home. Thus it seems appropriate, given Hardy's special feeling for this character, that she be the one allowed to enjoy a few months in circumstances that appear most thoroughly utopian as to their physical and social settings.

This is the period referred to in the novel as "The Rally," when Tess experiences the joys of labor and love in a neighborhood second in familiarity to Hardy to only the heath and the immediate surroundings of his birthplace. In the novel, this locale is called the Vale of the Great Dairies; in reality, it is the rich alluvial valley of the Frome River lying immediately south of the heath. Visually, it seems very different: attractive, fertile, and prosperous. Like the heath, however, it too provides an environment harmonious with the personalities and aspirations of its inhabitants. Upon first entering this region Tess "felt akin to the landscape."[7] Although she had grown up in an attractive dairying region some thirty miles northwest, Tess found the new, broader vistas "more cheering . . . . The new air was clear, bracing, ethereal. . . . The Frome waters were clear as the pure River of Life shown to the Evangelist. . . . Her hopes mingled with the sunshine in an ideal photosphere which surrounded her as she bounded along the soft south wind" (119). A short time later Hardy comments that she "had never in her recent life been so happy as she was now, possibly never would be so happy again. She was . . . physically and mentally suited among these new surroundings" (145).

Hardy heightens the perfection of this episode by stressing its associations with the Garden of Eden. This part of the novel covering the period from May through August, the months of greatest natural fecundity and which correlate with the increasing mutual attraction between Tess and Angel Clare. Hardy repeatedly presents their activities as part of the natural pattern of growth and fertility surrounding them. "Amid the oozing fatness and warm ferments of the Frome Vale at a season when the rush of juices could almost be heard below the hiss of fertilization it was impossible that the most fanciful love should not grow passionate. The ready bosoms existing there were impregnated by their late surroundings" (164). Sadly, in keeping with the novel's overall tone, the Vale also carries another Edenic association: impermanence. At most, it is a little over four months which see Tess regain her sense of worth and the start of what promises to be the positive relationship she so well deserves but is consistently and tragically denied.

The reason for this brevity points up another utopian quality of this period. Like so many schemes launched in the hopes of creating social perfection, the Tess-Angel relationship is based upon a misunderstanding of reality, in this case, their mutual inability to see each other's true nature. To Angel, Tess is his own "visionary essence of woman—a whole sex condensed into one typical form" (147). Tess first regards Angel as "an intelligence rather than as a man" (141), whom she later elevates to god-like status, unable to envision his fallibilities until she has over-confided in him.

The brutally fast way in which utopia can turn into dystopia is strikingly presented in *Tess*. After Tess and Angel separate, the novel jumps forward eight months to reveal Tess's fortunes on the downswing as she reaches the material and spiritual nadir of her life, a period in many respects the hellish counterpart of her days of bliss in the Vale of the Great Dairies.

Her sufferings at grim Flintcombe-Ash Farm last about five months, just slightly longer than her happiness at Talbothays Farm. Her utopia is experienced during the year's warmest months in fertile, low-lying country; her dystopia at the coldest time on high, barren ground. Whereas the vista around Talbothays was comprised of pleasantly diverse features—red and white cattle, green hedgerows, the clear river, golden sunlight—that at Flintcombe-Ash consists solely of outcrops of loose white flints and partly-eaten turnips:

> Every leaf of the vegetable having already been con-
> sumed, the whole field was in colour a desolate drab;
> it was a complexion without feature, as if a face from
> chin to brow, should be only an expanse of skin.
> The sky wore, in another colour, the same likeness; a
> white vacuity of countenance with the lineaments
> gone.

The disharmony of this landscape is brought out as Hardy presents its only visual features as grotesque and unnatural. The flints are described in a manner suggesting they are the weird fruits of this hostile region; they are "myriad in number" and in distinctly "bulbous, cusped, and phallic shapes" (303). Tess endures a winter there of exceptional bitterness and duration, characterized by frosts with unusually large crystals and violent snowstorms which send before them the strangest of birds:

> gaunt, spectral creatures with tragical eyes—eyes
> which had witnessed scenes of cataclysmal horror in
> inaccessible polar regions such as no human being
> had ever conceived. . . . half-blinded by the whirl
> of colossal storms and terraqueous distortions and
> [which] retained the expression of feature that such
> scenes had engendered. These nameless birds came
> quite close to Tess and [her friend] Marian, but of all

they had seen which humanity would never see, they
brought no account. (306)

The bleakness of the land is matched by the arduousness of
Tess's work: digging up and trimming the turnip-roots or, worse
yet, when outdoor labor is impossible, separating reeds from straw
in a barn. Her current employer is as despotic and sadistic as her
earlier boss was fair and benevolent.

To further remind the reader of the frightening contiguity of
these two extreme states, Hardy has Tess's friend Marian point out
that on a fine day one may see a hill just a few miles from
Talbothays. Also, the very presence of Marian, one of Tess's co-
workers at Talbothays, works in a similar fashion. The malevolence
of the Flintcombe-Ash environment brings about depression but not
despair in Tess and alcoholism in Marian.

Other dystopias in Hardy's fiction are also characterized by
distortion, barrenness, and inhospitality. In *Jude the Obscure,* such
landscapes are the result of so-called prosperity and expansion. A
good example is Stoke-Barehills, a characterless town which,
thanks to its strategic position near roads and railways, swells to
immense size during the annual agricultural show:

> It stands with its gaunt, unattractive, ancient church,
> and its new red-brick suburb, amid the open, chalk-
> soiled cornlands. . . . The most familiar object in
> Stoke-Barehills nowadays is its cemetery, standing
> among some picturesque medieval ruins beside the
> railway; the modern chapels, modern tombs, and
> modern shrubs having a look of intrusiveness amid
> the crumbling and ivy-covered decay of the ancient
> walls. (284–85)

As in most of the novel, little of benefit to the protagonist occurs
when he visits the fair. *Jude* is Hardy's last and most dystopian
novel; nowhere can Jude and the woman he loves fit in, due in part
to their *avant-garde* attitudes toward education and marriage. The
new versus old dichotomy which eventually helps destroy both protagonists is mirrored in the novel's rural and urban settings by the
juxtaposition of new and old architectural elements. In Jude's sleepy
home village of Marygreen, the ancient church

60

> hump-backed, wood-turreted, and quaintly hipped,
> had been taken down and either cracked up into
> heaps of road-metal in the lane, or utilized as pig-sty
> walls, garden seats, guard-stones to fences, and
> rockeries in the flower-beds of the neighborhood. In
> place of it a tall new building of modern Gothic de-
> sign, unfamiliar to English eyes, had been erected on
> a new piece of ground by a certain obliterator of his-
> toric records who had run down from London and
> back in a day. (16)

In this backwater, Jude is prominent in only an eccentric way,
known to all as the young man who creates a road hazard by study-
ing Latin and Greek while driving a delivery-wagon. Later, Jude's
inability to realize his educational goals at Christminster (Oxford) is
hauntingly epitomized by his lodgings in the working-class Victorian suburbs, from which he can see, even walk through, the clois-
tered medieval quadrangles which forever shut him out.

Other characters' frustrations are similarly presented against a
new-old cultural disjunction. Sue Bridehead, the object of Jude's
affections, marries instead a middle-aged schoolteacher named Phillotson and joins him in the hilltop village of Shaston (Shaftesbury).
Introducing Shaston, Hardy contrasts its near mythical Anglo-Saxon
and medieval glories—a castle, abbey, twelve churches, a mint,
tombs of royalty and of martyrs—with its modern reputation as a
center for laziness and moral laxity, underscored by its popularity as
a winter haven for circuses, side shows, and other purveyors of eccentricity. Sadly, the relationship between Sue and Phillotson is
presented in a series of almost comic episodes where Sue's sexual
squeamishness and Phillotson's humane acceptance of her problem
stand apart from middle-class sexual mores as do the show people
from the natives of Shaston. The identification of Sue and Phillotson
with these social outcasts is clearly made when they loudly and vio-
lently side with the couple during the public meeting called to discuss Phillotson's dismissal.

The final example of a dystopian landscape in *Jude* gains much
of its painful power from its earlier being the novel's one near-
utopian setting. This is the high ground crossed by an ancient thor-
oughfare called the Ridgeway near a milestone and a barn. Here,
like Hardy on the heath, young Jude can both escape the frustrations

of the everyday world and, by climbing atop the old barn (known as the Brown House), catch a glimpse of the turrets and spires of Christminster, beacons to an enchanted citadel of learning which, Jude concludes, "would just suit me" (30). On one occasion, he crystallizes his desires by carving the word "Thither" and his initials on the milestone. It is thus grimly appropriate that just as this setting is associated with the nurture of his goals that it be later entwined with not only the death of his dreams but also of Jude himself.

Later in the novel, Jude makes one last unsuccessful attempt to persuade Sue out of further punishing herself through a loveless reconciliation with Phillotson. At this time the couple are living back in Marygreen, a five-mile walk over the hills from the nearest railway station. Jude makes the trip in poor health during a chilly November rainstorm. He reaches the village through sheer determination, but after Sue refuses to alter her decision, Jude's death-sentence seems to be meted out by the same landscape which earlier held out so much promise:

> There are cold spots up and down Wessex in autumn and winter weather; but the coldest of all when a north or east wind is blowing is the crest of the down by the Brown House, where the road to Alfredston crosses the old Ridgeway. Here the first winter sleets and snows fall and lie, and here the spring frost lingers last unthawed. Here in the teeth of the northeast wind and rain Jude now pursued his way, wet through, the necessary slowness of his walk from lack of his former strength being insufficient to maintain his heat. He came to the milestone . . . spread his blanket and lay down there to rest. Before moving on he went and felt at the back of the stone for his own carving. It was still there; but nearly obliterated by moss. . . . To get home he had to travel by a steam tram-car, and two branches of railway with much waiting at a junction. He did not reach Christminster until ten o'clock. (385–86)

To find an environment which for Hardy himself was dystopian, it helps to review the chief attributes of his utopias: physical congruity, which in turn fostered individual fulfillment and social harmony in a setting where man was numerically insignificant. The opposite of these qualities typifies much of the London scene with which Hardy was quite familiar, having lived there from 1862–67, 1875–76, and 1878–81. Periods of shorter residency and brief business visits occurred in nearly every other year of his adulthood until 1885, when he built a permanent home in the county town of Dorchester, three miles from his birthplace. From then on he spent his annual social season in London (about four months), a habit kept up until 1911 when Hardy was seventy years old. His letters, autobiography, and memoranda leave no doubt that he much enjoyed the wealth of social and cultural contacts his fame afforded, but his observations on the city itself reveal a deep-seated distress with the realities of urban life and its effect on the individual.

Physical distortion and violent contrast are key elements in many of Hardy's observations about London. The sun on a winter day is described as "a red-hot bullet hanging in a livid atmosphere —reflected from window panes in the form of bleared copper eyes, and inflaming the sheets of plateglass with smears of gory light. A drab snow mingled itself with liquid horsedung, and in the river puddings of ice moved slowly on."[8] At Piccadilly Circus, a nocturnal gathering place for persons of ill repute, Hardy noted, " . . . among all the wily crew, there was a little innocent family standing waiting, I suppose for an omnibus. How pure they looked! A man on a stretcher, with a bloody bandage round his head, was wheeled past by two policeman, stragglers following. Such is Piccadilly" (235). On another occasion Hardy saw a large carriage forcing its way through a crowded street and containing "the *petite* figure of the owner's young wife . . . slim, small; who could be easily carried under a man's arm, and who, if held up by the hair and slipped out of her clothes, carriage, etc., would not be much larger than a skinned rabbit, and of less use" (237). At the Empire Music Hall, Hardy viewed the dancing girls as "nearly all skeletons. One can see drawn lines and puckers in their young flesh. They should be penned and fattened for a month to round out their beauty" (251).

A number of Hardy's most powerful comments about London employ distortion along with a personal trait that made it difficult for him to enjoy life in any city: distaste of crowds and physical contact. Hardy did not like being touched, admitting ". . . to the end of his life he disliked even the most friendly hand being laid on his arm or shoulder" (25). In 1879 Hardy and his wife viewed the dense crowds assembled for a parade. To her, "the surface of the crowd seemed like a boiling cauldron of porridge." Hardy's impression was much more ominous:

> As the crowd grows denser it loses its character of an aggregate of countless units, and becomes an organic whole, a molluscous black creature having nothing in common with humanity, that takes the shape of the streets along which it has lain itself, and throws out horrid excrescences and limbs into neighboring alleys; a creature whose voice exudes from its scaly coat and who has an eye in every pore of its body. The balconies, stands, and railway-bridge are occupied by small detached shapes of the same tissue, but of gentler motion, as if they were the spawn of the monster in their midst. (131)

For Hardy, population statistics could arouse horror. On May 19, 1879, he recorded that he could not sleep owing to an eerie feeling which possessed him, "a horror at lying down in close proximity to a monster who had four million heads and eight million eyes" (137).

Far from promoting harmony between the individual and his environment, London life for Hardy had ill effects both physical and psychological. Although the illness which in 1867 sent Hardy home from London was brought on by personal disappointments as well as by polluted air and ineffective sanitation, later periods spent in London nearly always enervated him or brought on an attack of influenza. More serious and more vividly denounced by Hardy was the city's destruction of individual personalities and people's sense of interdependence.

As early as 1872, when planning a business trip there, he felt the need to "stifle his constitutional tendency to care for life only as emotion and not as a scientific game" (87). Shortly after Hardy's marriage in 1874, a fellow novelist wrote to him, "I hear that you are coming to live in stony-hearted London. Our great fault is that we are all alike. . . . We press so closely against each other that any small shoots are cut off at once, and the young tree grows in shape like the old one" (101). Hardy included these comments in his autobiography.

He used a different metaphor when in 1892 he expressed relief at leaving the metropolis "and all those dinners. London, that *hot-plate* of humanity on which we first sing, then simmer, then boil, then dry away to dust and ashes" (246–47). By this time, of course, Hardy enjoyed the financial independence to sample only those aspects of urban life that he wished and to leave it when he chose, a freedom unavailable to the vast majority of Londoners. While waiting for his wife at a busy intersection near Hyde Park, he declared,

> This hum of the wheel, the roar of London! What is it composed of? Hurry, speech, laughter, moans, cries of little children. The people in this tragedy laugh, sing, smoke, toss off wines, etc., make love to girls in drawing rooms and areas, and yet are playing their parts in the tragedy just the same. All are caged birds; the only difference lies in the size of the cage. (171)

Several times Hardy remarked upon how urban life causes individuals to retreat into their own separate worlds focused only upon immediate needs:

> London appears not to *see itself*. Each individual is conscious of *himself* but nobody conscious of themselves collectively, except perhaps some poor gaper who stares round with a half-idiotic aspect. There is no consciousness here of where anything comes from or goes to—only that it is present . . . . The fiendish precision or mechanism of town life is what makes it so intolerable to the sick or infirm. Like acrobats performing on a succession of swinging trapezes, so long as you are at particular points at precise instances, everything glides as if afloat, but if you are not up to time—. (206–07)

That Hardy nowhere offered a contrasting urban picture bears out the validity of viewing him as a "sympathetic realist." Most of these dystopian features of late Victorian London are still very much with us: the schedule-conscious corporate struggle for survival, depersonalization, and alienation. Though he would continue to abhor such values, Hardy today would find much with which he was familiar in the urban scene of 1984.

NOTES

[1] Both passages cited by F. B. Pinion, *A Hardy Companion* (London: Macmillan, 1974) 178–79.

[2] F. E. Hardy, *The Life of Thomas Hardy* (London: Macmillan, 1962; first pub. in 2 vols. 1928, 1930) 116, 120. Though the name of Hardy's second wife appears on the title page, the *Life* is recognized as Hardy's autobiography. All page references are to the one-volume edition.

[3] *Thomas Hardy's Wessex* (London: Macmillan, 1983), 17.

[4] *Jude the Obscure* (London, 1895; rpt. New York: New American Library, 1961) 22. All page references are to this edition; the same procedure is followed with other Hardy novels cited later.

[5] *The Complete Poems of Thomas Hardy,* ed. James Gibson (London: Macmillan, 1976) 864.

[6] *The Return of the Native* (London, 1878; rpt. New York: New American Library, 1959) 11–12.

[7] *Tess of the d'Urbervilles* (London, 1891; rpt. New York: New American Library, 1964) 118 .

[8] *The Life of Thomas Hardy,* 232. All page references are to this edition.

7. CHILDHOOD'S END: APOCALYPTIC RESOLUTION IN *CANDIDE*

JoAnn James

"TULIT ERGO DOMINUS DEUS hominem et posuit eum in paradiso voluptatis ut operaretur et custodiret illum."[1] Despite the images of violence and despair that occur in Voltaire's "conte philosophique" *Candide,* the sustained thematic image present in the text is that of the "earthly Paradise" or garden.[2] Variations of this image serve as objective correlatives to the four major fictional modes that inform the narrative: the picaresque novel, the traveler's tale, the quest romance, and the *Bildungsroman.* The geographic, experiential, mythic, and philosophic trajectories that express these modes within the text impart its particular resonance and significance.[3] Candide's journey from Westphalia to "our garden" on the shores of the Propontis brings him from childhood innocence to maturity, from exile to the foundation of a new social order, from blind faith to the formulation of a new and unique commandment.

"Once upon a time in Westphalia . . ."
Candide's journey begins, as does each individual's,[4] with the loss of innocence, the sudden exile from "paradis terrestre."[5] Although this phrase does not occur until the beginning of the second chapter, the reader can have no doubt of the intended location. In the course of centuries and a geographic shift of site from the fertile

67

Tigris-Euphrates valley to the barren plains of Westphalia, which Voltaire had traversed in his journey to Berlin in 1750, it is evident that both Paradise and its inhabitants have fallen from grace. Voltaire's opinion of Westphalia is succinctly expressed in his correspondence: "Quel chien de pays que la Westphalia."[6]

God's presence in the garden is replaced in Westphalia by the "thundering" baron. The patriarchal creation myth is ironically undermined by the addition of the ponderous, Venus-of-Willendorf baroness. Eve-Cunégonde glows with the robust, nubile charms of a milkmaid—charms perhaps somewhat ill-suited to her future role as quest princess as they certainly are to her saintly namesake whose place in the martyrology of the Roman Catholic church was won by a fervid defense of her chastity. The mystery surrounding the birth of Adam-Candide reveals his identity as both the "orphan, half-outsider, . . . unfortunate traveler" of Guillén's picaresque code[7] and the "fatherless son of a royal virgin" listed in Raglan's construct of the "hero's pedigree."[8]

The expulsion of man from Paradise is attributed by Saint Thomas Aquinas to "concupiscence—the rise of inordinate desire."[9] Although the seduction of Eve may have been metaphysical, arousing only her *libido scienti,* such is not the case of Paquette, Cunégonde's understudy. Paquette's "leçon de physique expérimentale" is personally administered by Pangloss, cast as the serpent in the garden whose wily tongue had deceived Eve in Eden. Pangloss is also revealed as the Great Deceiver, the Adversary who seeks to impose upon the innocent Candide the fatalistic philosophy of optimism which would keep him forever in the garden, an eternal adolescent never attempting to attain autonomy, happy to obey the baron and admire Cunégonde, never seeking the freedom to assign a meaning, essence, to his own existence beyond that imposed upon him. And what of the fair Cunégonde? Having witnessed with voyeuristic pleasure Paquette's reiterated lessons, she is now filled with an immoderate desire to become as learned *(savante)* as Paquette; through, upon, beneath what Tree of Knowledge we may well imagine. Seducing Candide, Cunégonde assumes Eve's primal guilt for man's Fortunate Fall. So it is that Candide and Cunégonde find themselves, and are found by the wrathful baron, behind the screen where forbidden fruits are most certainly being fondled if not ingested. So the first garden is lost.

The garden of Westphalia belongs to the picaresque mode,

situated midway between comedy and satire,[10] positing an exterior world of disjunction and destruction. Kicked into a reality of absurdity and chaos, Candide is "embarked"[11] upon the picaro's horizontal (geographic) and vertical (social) journeys, upon the hero's quest to marry the princess and gain the kingdom, upon the individual's search for psychic wholeness and a coherent meaning for existence, upon the testing of the truth of Pangloss's oracular declaration: "Ceux qui ont avancé que tout est bien ont dit une sottise: il fallait dire que tout est au mieux" (180).

Outside Paradise, Candide's disastrous adventures propel him, one into another, at a bewildering pace. The chapter titles accent the episodic narrative: "Ce que devint Candide parmi les Bulgares" (181), ". . . Le Docteur Pangloss, et ce qui en advint" (185), "Comment une Vieille prit soin de Candide, et comment il retrouva ce qu'il aimait" (191), "Histoire de Cunégonde" (193). The titles divide the narration between misfortunes experienced and a contrapuntal recital of those exterior but not extraneous to Candide's personal circumstances. Fortuitous encounters abound, as the reader would expect; each such encounter reveals an extraordinary physical or moral deterioration in the person encountered. Only Candide, like the tarot's Fool, remains relatively unscathed.

Pangloss is now half-blind, a consequence of love's lessons. (The reader might anticipate that a philosophical eye opening has occurred as a result of this incident, a Tiresian insight achieved, but Pangloss's spirited defense of syphilis as "indispensable dans le meilleur des mondes" (186) proves that there are none so blind as philosophers.) Mlle. Cunégonde, already "violée autant qu'on peut l'être" (185), shares her considerable favors, mediating them structurally between a Jewish banker and the Grand Inquisitor. La Vieille has already lost half her . . . life in slavery, white and multicolored.

Through earthquake and auto-da-fé, through wars and their attendant evils: "Les vieillards criblés de coups, . . . leurs femmes égorgées, . . . des filles éventrées après avoir assouvi les besoins naturels de quelques héros" (183), Candide makes his way, experiencing the Old World as dystopia, daring finally, as he sets sail for the New World, to admit the undeniable existence in Europe of "le mal physique et . . . le mal moral qui couvrent la terre et la mer" (204). This first independent judgment based on his own experience marks the end of Candide's total philosophical innocence. The crossing of the sea is that rite of initiation that permits entry into a new Paradise.

"Finally there was a prairie . . ."

If the Old World is firmly in the throes of metaphysical and physical evil, man and nature may have fared better in the unspoiled natural beauty of the New World, rumored site of a utopian golden land, goal of travelers, soldiers, and soldiers of fortune since the days of the conquistadors. Candide disembarks, filled with new hope: "C'est certainement le nouveau monde qui est le meilleur des univers possibles" (198). Voltaire encourages reader expectation that this may be the case by trebling the gardens found there: the kingdom of the Jesuits in Paraguay, the country of the Oreillons, and Eldorado. Here the picaro's travels are enriched by the literary tradition of the traveler's tale which recounts fantastic, often imaginary, exotic marvels. A staple of popular literature since the *Odyssey,* revived during the Renaissance, especially by Rabelais, the traveler's tale during the seventeenth century and the Enlightenment was frequently associated with the theme of utopia.[12]

In the New World there is an amelioration to be noted. The natural disasters which plague the Old World, piously known as "acts of God," do not occur. It is European *man* who has brought his old vices to the new continent. The Spanish, the Portuguese, and the Dutch have despoiled nature's goodness. However abundant nature's produce, man's greed surpasses its bounty.

Paraguay, a Jesuit theocracy, might have preserved its primal innocence, its "noble savages" tilling an irenic garden under the pastoral protection of God's ministers. Instead, as Cacambo tells his master: "Los Padres y ont tout, et les peuples rien: c'est le chef-d'oeuvre de la raison et de la justice" (207). The natives of Eden have been enslaved by priest and planter (in Surinam); the produce of their land and labor nourishes their exploiters and provides exotic delicacies which grace the tables of their masters. In this post-Edenic world fieldwork is a curse, and meager nourishment is earned in the sweat of the laborer's brow.[13]

Despite the social injustice to which he is witness in Paraguay, Candide might have found his personal "paradis terrestre" here; reunited with Cunégonde, sharing the sumptuous life of the Jesuits, warmly welcomed by Cunégonde's brother whose novel experiences during the rape of his father's castle have presumably left him with a taste for Bulgarian buggery shared by his fellow Jesuits: "Quel plaisir los Padres auront quand ils sauront qu'il leur vient un capitaine qui sait l'exercice bulgare!" (207). However, Candide is forced to bare his sword precipitously and run the young baron through when the latter is roused to anger at Candide's proposal to wed Cunégonde and her "soixante et douze quartiers" (210) as soon as they can be wrested from the governor of Buenos Aires. And so Candide is forced to flee the New World's first garden, God's soldiers yapping at his heels.

And what of "pure nature"? Somewhere on this vast new continent virgin forests and verdant fields must flourish. Fleeing the Jesuits, Candide and Cacambo enter a luxuriant prairie where the land of the Oreillons borders on that of Los Padres.[14] Travelers ever, they pause, stunned at the exotic drama that unfolds before them as naked maidens flee their later-to-be-revealed simian suitors. Denounced by the disappointed damsels for the murder of the amorous anthropoids, Candide and Cacambo are captured and about to be consumed by the Oreillons, who have taken a liking for spit-roasted Jesuits. Candide is freed upon the revelation that, although he is robed like a Jesuit, "l'habit ne fait pas le moine." Encouraged by the eminently rational behavior of these "savages," Candide takes joyous leave of the Oreillons, voicing a positive, if naive, judgment on his experience: "Mais, après tout, la pure nature est bonne" (214).

"A country that surpasses Westphalia . . ."

In an abandoned canoe, afloat on an unknown river, pushed forward by the current,[15] Candide and Cacambo happen upon the New World's ultimate garden, Eldorado. This is surely nature's authentic Paradise: "où le pays était cultivé pour le plaisir comme pour le besoin" (215).

The land is inhabited by a people of wondrous beauty who reflect the beauty of the world about them. Here roads are pebbled with precious stones and golden nuggets. Roadside inns spread their tables with cloth of gold and nourish travelers on the government's expense account. Extravagant luxury adorns the house of every citizen. The contrast between the castle of Thunder-ten-tronckh and the house of the retired court official in Eldorado demonstrates the almost incomprehensible disjunction between the outside world and this enclosed and privileged land: "Monsieur le baron était un des plus puissants seigneurs de la Vestphalie, car son château avait une porte et des fenêtres. Sa grande salle même était ornée d'une tapisserie" (179); and

> Ils entrèrent dans une maison fort simple, car la porte n'était que d'argent, et les lambris des appartements n'étaient que d'or, mais travaillés avec tant de goût que les plus riches lambris ne l'effaçaient pas. L'antichambre n'était à la vérité incrustée que de rubis et d'émeraudes; mais l'ordre dans lequel tout était arrangé réparait bien cette extrême simplicité. (217)

Here no criminal disturbs civil tranquility, no clash of religious dogma sets brother against brother, no war has ever brought catastrophic suffering to the nation. Here a happy, prosperous people give themselves to the worship of God and the cultivation of their land, scientific inquiry, and the art of living well. It is, in very fact, the utopia of which Western man has dreamed from the Republic of Plato to the Big Rock Candy Mountain of American folklore, but is it Paradise enow?

In Eldorado God, man, and nature live in harmony and hyperbolic plenty. Candide recognizes that this is probably the unique land so favored: "C'est probablement le pays où tout va bien, car il faut absolument qu'il y en ait un de cette espèce. Et quoi qu'en dit maître Pangloss, je me suis souvent aperçu que tout allait mal en Vestphalie" (217).

Eldorado is also a prison-house, however fair. No citizen may ever leave. Will another stranger ever enter? Is life lived at stasis-point endless happiness or is it endless ennui? Can happiness be given to man by God or nature, or must he wrest it from his fate in unequal battle? La Vieille's ultimate question has already been asked.

Candide and Cacambo flee bountiful, beautiful Eldorado with happy heart, eager to continue the quest for Cunégonde, anticipating the pleasure of causing immeasurable envy because of their vast, newly acquired riches, and, true to the tradition of travel literature, determined "à faire parade de ce qu'on a vu dans ses voyages" (220). They have judged nature's finest garden and found it wanting.

The abrupt fall into reality occurs on the road to Surinam.

Candide and Cacambo encounter the mutilated slave, tragic symbol of Western man's exploitation and destruction of the paradisiacal New World and the enslavement of Adam's "cousins issus de germain" (222). This abrupt juxtaposition of utopia and dystopia closes the travel narrative, returning Candide and reader to the picaro's world. With Cacambo and Martin, Candide sets sail for Europe and an anticipated reunion with the quest princess, Cunégonde.

Candide is rooted in the experiential as well as in literary traditions and archetypes. Voltaire now propels Candide at dizzying pace through contemporary Europe, adding to the picaresque novel a roman à clef. Always in the right place at the right time to witness some new absurdity in this world of dupes and scoundrels, Candide visits Paris where the body of an adored actress cannot be buried in hallowed ground, and the author settles old scores with literary critics and rivals; the shores of England where he witnesses the execution of an admiral for having lost a battle; Venice where he makes the acquaintance of the disillusioned dilettante, Pococurante, who has read everything and appreciated nothing; and finally, Constantinople where the lovers will be reunited with each other, "tout le monde et son petit frère."

Childhood's End

In the garden of the *metairie,* purchased by Candide and inhabited by the little band of Westphalians and friends, a band of survivors who have "come through," all ends and all begins. Picaro, traveler, and hero have finished their journey. The callow youth has matured; the picaro has attained position in society; the traveler has seen what the world has to offer; the hero has attained a kingdom and the hand of his long-desired, somewhat-altered bride.

But the hero has yet another role—to establish a new order, bringing peace and plenty to his people. And all is not well at the *metairie.* Greetings over and personal adventures exchanged, wearied by long discussion between Pangloss and his foil Martin, in touch with the tumultuous outside world only through what can be seen from the windows of the farmhouse, Candide and his band are safe, well nourished, together, and utterly, irremediably bored. Cunégonde becomes daily more shrewish; Paquette can no longer ply her trade. Martin is silent and despairs. Faithful Cacambo toils in the vegetable patch and curses his fate. It is La Vieille who dares ask the overwhelming question:

> Je voudrais savoir lequel est le pire, où d'être at-
> taquée cent fois par des pirates nègres, de passer par
> les baguettes chez les Bulgares, d'être fouetté et pen-
> du dans un auto-da-fé, d'être disséqué, de ramer aux
> galères, d'éprouver enfin toutes les misères par les-
> quelles nous avons tous passé, ou bien de rester ici à
> ne rien faire. (257)

Consultation with a dervish "qui passait pour le meilleur philosophe de la Turquie" (257), brings only a partial answer to the
question—not to question. It is the example of an anonymous "bon
vieillard,"[16] encountered by chance, that provides Candide with the
ritual key to the kingdom, the revealing vision which will permit the
hero to redeem his disciples and bestow upon them peace and reconciliation, meld them into a society.

Pondering on the old man's revelation of his formula for happiness, "Je . . . cultive [mes vingt arpents de terre] avec mes en-
fants; le travail éloigne de nous trois grands maux, l'ennui, le vice,
et le besoin" (258), Candide formulates a new and unique commandment: "Il faut cultiver notre jardin" (259). Here Candide, the
third Adam, inaugurates a new secular order. The condescending
imperatives of the Decalogue are replaced by the statement of a joint
duty—"Il faut." The duty is to preserve and improve the earth we
share—"cultiver." The earth is fertile and nourishing—"notre jardin." Neither spiritual obedience nor faith binds us here, as in the
gardens of the first and second Adams,[17] but the revelation/recogni-
tion of our symbiotic tie. We are for the garden and the garden is for
us. "Notre jardin" is not utopia but it can become a place of transformation where man in cooperation with nature can mediate their
absurd disjunction. If the *lacrimae rerum* of man's nature prevent his
total happiness, he can achieve contentment, self-respect, and a degree of control over his own existence.

Without the "cultivation" of our mind, will, and hand, the
dystopias of the Old and New World will endlessly repeat: "'tis an
unweeded garden / That grows to seed: things rank and gross in nature / Possess it merely." Freed at last from the illusion of perfecti-
bility as well as from the quagmire of despair, Candide is at childhood's end—where there are no final answers. But then, this is only
the beginning.[18]

NOTES

¹ *Biblia Sacra, iuxta vulgatam versione* (Stuttgart: Deutsche Bibelgesellschaft, 1983), I, Genesis 2:17.
² The word "Paradise" is derived from the Greek of the *Septuaguint* from Persian. It means an "enclosed garden." See also: Bottiglia, W. F. "Voltaire's *Candide* : Analysis of a Classic" in *Studies on Voltaire and the XVIII Century*, t VII, 2nd edition (Geneva: 1964).
³ On reading for thematic significance, see Jonathan Culler, "Literary Competence," *Structuralist Poetics* (Ithaca, New York: Cornell University Press, 1975) 113–30.
⁴ J. E. Cirlot, "Paradise Lost," *A Dictionary of Symbols*, trans. Jack Sage (New York: Philosophical Library, 1971) 249–50.
⁵ Voltaire, *Candide ou l'Optimisme* in *Romans et Contes,* ed. René Pomeau (Paris: Garnier-Flammarion, 1966) 181. All references are to this edition.
⁶ Voltaire, *Candide ou l'Optimisme,* ed. George Havens (New York: Henry Holt and Company, 1951) 114, quoting from Morland, *Oeuvres complétes de Voltaire,* XXXVII 146.
⁷ Claudio Gullén, *Literature as System* (Princeton: University Press, 1971).
⁸ Lord Ragland, *The Hero* (New York: Vintage Books, 1956) 174–5.
⁹ *The Catholic Encyclopedia,* comp. Robert C. Broderick (Nashville: Thomas Nelson, Inc., 1975) 440.
¹⁰ Robert Scholes, *Structuralism in Literature* (New Haven and London: Yale University Press, 1974) 134–8.
¹¹ As Camus characterized the contemporary condition in accepting the Nobel Prize for Literature, 1957.
¹² Hans-Gunter Funke, "Zur Geschichte Utopias: Ansätze auf klaerischen Fortschirittsdenks in der französeschen Reiseutopie des 17 Jahrhunderts," in Wilhelm Vosskamp, ed. *Utopieforschung: Interdisziplnäre Studien zur neuzeitlichen Utopie,*II (Stuttgart: Netzler, 1982) 299–319.
¹³ *Biblia*, Genesis 3:11–19. Note also Pangloss's mistranslation of the earlier passage from Genesis in which he translates "ut opera-

retur . . . illum" (supra 1) as "pour qu'il travailât" (259).

[14] From the Spanish name for a tribe of South American Indians, the *Orejones,* who distended their ears by piercing them with large wooden plugs.

[15] Note the author's repeated indications that Eldorado is found only when Candide has temporarily abandoned any attempt to direct the quest.

[16] Voltaire himself? The author had already found delight in gardening at Les Délices in 1755 and later at Ferney became interested in new methods of cultivation. Contemporary interest in agriculture is amply demonstrated in the *Enclyclopédie.* The extended sense is, of course, also understood.

[17] Christ, as the second Adam, opens Paradise to man and on the cross calls the "good thief" to share Paradise (the state of heavenly bliss) with him "this day."

[18] As the countless farms, cooperatives, and communes from that day to this attest (e.g., Brook Farm, Walden II, and Soleri's beautiful Arcosanti).

8. *INDIA SONG/LE VICE CONSUL* OF MARGUERITE DURAS: COMPARATIVE TECHNIQUES IN FILM AND NOVEL

Patricia Struebig

INDIA SONG/LE VICE CONSUL of Marguerite Duras, as novel, screentext, and film present some curious and striking resemblances and contrasts which lead to the proposal of new deductions concerning the Vice-consul's "story." Critics have discussed Marguerite Duras's skill as a producer of films derived from her own novels,[1] analyzed thematic similarities in a series of related works,[2] described the function of the multiple and constantly mobile points of view in the art of this novelist.[3] They have not, however, made a comparative analysis of the methods of presenting similar elements on paper and on the screen, to find the resulting differences in audience perception of this material. This study proposes to analyze such aspects of *India Song* and *Le Vice-Consul,* and to indicate varying interpretations which result from: 1) reading a novel written as a novel, 2) reading a screentext based on similar information used in the earlier novel, and 3) viewing the film which actually results from this screentext.

It is important first to indicate agreement with Alfred Cismaru, Carol Murphy and other critics[4] who speak of the clear thematic repetitions in *Le Ravissement de Lol V. Stein, L'Amour, La Femme du Gange, Le Vice-Consul,* and *India Song.* All of these works— some novels, some screentexts—are related by the reappearance of several characters and by some plot and setting similarities. None of the works contains all of the same material, but are, to adopt a structuralist expression, different "versions" of the tale. According to Claude Lévi-Strauss, none of the versions of a tale will contain all the information necessary to clearly relate its meaning, but a comparison of differences or lacks in the versions will point out the sometimes deliberately obscured meaning.[5] It is, in fact, the differences between the versions of the story of *India Song/Le Vice-Consul* which we seek here.

The characters Anne-Marie Stretter and Michael Richardson initially appear in *Le Ravissement de Lol V. Stein,* the 1964 novel.[6] Our reference to this work stops here, with the establishment of their relationship as lovers irrevocably bound from the moment of their first encounter. Passion between them, however, is never overtly mentioned, nor is it intrinsic to the understanding of *India Song/Le Vice-Consul* as some critics believe.[7]

In the next version, the 1965 novel *Le Vice-Consul,*[8] these two characters return, surrounded by the others who will amplify the tale. The Vice-consul of Lahore, Jean-Marc de H., makes his appearance here. Guilty of shooting the lepers in the Shalimar Gardens in Lahore, he is removed from his post and sent to the embassy in Calcutta; he is condemned more by his anti-social behavior in acting against the social indifference of the white community than he is by his criminal act.[9] Michael Richardson (of *Lol V. Stein)* becomes Michael Richard, a businessman who met Anne-Marie Stretter in Calcutta and now makes his home there, never to depart:

> ... je l'entendais jouer à Calcutta, le soir, sur le
> boulevard; ça m'intriguait beaucoup, je ne savais pas
> qui elle était, j'étais venu en touriste à Calcutta, je me
> souviens, je ne tenais pas du tout le coup ... je
> voulais repartir dès le premier jour, et ... c'est
> elle, cette musique que j'entendais qui fait que je suis
> resté—que ... j'ai pu rester à Calcutta ....
> (VC, 187)

Also introduced are: The Ambassador of France to Calcutta, husband of Anne-Marie Stretter; George Crawn (the same Georges Crawn of *India Song),* businessman and long-time friend (perhaps former lover) of Anne-Marie Stretter (VC, 187); the writer, Peter

Morgan, also a business associate of Crawn and Richard, who plans to tell a story (yet another, future version of this tale) about the Indian beggarwoman and Anne-Marie Stretter; and Charles Rossett, the young attaché to the French Embassy and newest addition to the group of admirers of this striking woman. The beggarwoman is also present and the reader learns her tale as the stories of the two women are linked and conjectured upon throughout the development of this version.

L'Amour, the 1972 novel, and *La Femme du Gange,* the 1973 film,[10] take up the life of Lol V. Stein after her madness has returned. These are very limited versions which do not add to our knowledge of the Vice-consul's story, but rather continue the tale after his role has ended. They do, however, substantiate one of the main differences between the written texts of *Le Vice-Consul* and *India Song.* In *Le Vice-Consul,* Anne-Marie Stretter does not die. She is last pictured, robed in black, stretched out in the pathway at the residence of the French Embassy in the Delta Islands, and only perhaps swimming in the dark waters of the sea—this, in a dream version of Charles Rossett. *India Song* clearly states that she dies there, that night, on the Delta:

Voix I

. . . morte là-bas?

Voix II
Aux îles. (Hésitation) Trouvée morte. Une nuit. [11]

And in *La Femme du Gange* it is stated that, after the death of Anne-Marie Stretter, "Le Voyageur" (Michael Richardson) was married and had two children. [12]

Chronologically in the works of the author, we have arrived at the time of writing *India Song,* 1974. Here we have all the characters mentioned in the previous works, but Peter Morgan is simply "L'Invité des Stretter" (IS, 46 and 107). Michael Richardson again possesses the past given him in *Le Ravissement de Lol V. Stein* (IS, 15).

What we seek now are contrastive elements in the presentations of this information. Changes in factual details among the versions are few and have little overall consequence to the tale. There are, however, areas of major importance which by definition must be treated differently from paper to movie screen: the themes of Love, equated with life, and Non-Love, eventually equated with death, and the leitmotifs of music and heat.

All the versions of the tale are variations on the theme of Love; L'Amour with a capital *A*. Each character and each relationship represents another aspect of Love, with *India Song,* the film, being the most all-encompassing syntagm of the "love story."

The woman, Anne-Marie Stretter, the music "India Song," the Vice-consul, all of the men attracted to Anne-Marie Stretter, the lepers, the beggarwoman, the "grumbling and grinding" of Calcutta—noises which represent the masses of India in film and novel—symbolize Love, and life, on both paper and screen. The film, however, uses sight and sound to offer a spectrum of scenes and static poses accompanied by music, voices, noises, the suggestion of odor through sight and sound, which effectively act upon the viewer's subconscious to evoke actions and awaken knowledge which must be consciously explained by words on paper in the written versions.

The novel *Le Vice-Consul* is sufficient in itself to present the background to the story and to relate the tale of the Vice-consul and his crime. In truth, one knows more facts after reading this novel than after viewing the film *India Song*. Many details which are clarified in *Le Vice-Consul* remain on a symbolic level in *India Song*. For example, in the novel, the reader understands the role of *India Song'*s "Invité," who is a silent observer, "un figurant," in the movie, but a participant, the writer Peter Morgan, in the earlier novel. The reader can also comprehend by words on paper the Vice-consul's crime and the reason for the atmosphere of unspoken horror and the consequent problem of adjustment common to the "whites" in India. These elements are important to understand the "story" of the Vice-consul.

To understand the meaning of the story, one must search on other levels. The film permits the senses of sight and hearing to record information not available on paper which is then unconsciously assimilated by the viewer and thus allowed to signify on a different plane. One reads the words "dans les jardins, il sifflote 'India Song'" (VC, 147), and "Anne-Marie Stretter joue le Schubert .... La phrase musicale est déjà deux fois revenue. La voici pour la troisième fois. On attend qu'elle revienne encore. La voici" (VC, 162). And one reads over and over again in both *Le Vice Consul* and *India Song:* "Il l'invite à danser. . . , ils dansent, . . .

80

il va danser, . . . " (VC, 106–122 passim). "Ils dansent lente-ment, dansent." "Le soir, ils dansaient . . .", "Ils se rapprochent dans la danse jusqu'à ne faire qu'un. 'India Song' s'éloigne" (IS, 18–20 passim). But hearing the actual repetition of the haunting melody of 'India Song' and observing the continual flux of dancing couples gives meaning to the words.

Anne-Marie Stretter in her gaunt beauty, white-skinned, robed in black, is nearly immobile, a posed statue of a woman. She be-comes a Figura, symbolic of Life, Love, Death, all of these in one —India. This conclusion can be drawn after careful readings of the several texts, but is made astonishingly evident in the film by her visual representation on the screen and the consequent association of this Figura with music in general and with the "India Song" in particular.

She is viewed as the past and present recipient—immobile, ungiving, unsharing—of the love of many men, old and young. These male characters in the film *India Song* are less defined than in the novel *Le Vice-Consul,* for they also are symbolic of Love. Their true roles are not those of ambassador, vice-consul, businessman, writer, attaché, but rather of "lovers." Thus, all attention is again di-rected to the Figura of Anne-Marie Stretter: "Toute l'Inde Blanche les regarde" (VC, 121).

To the eyes of the viewer she does not, however, become "In-dia" as clearly as on paper. That the love she embodies is all-en-compassing, that of all human existence, is felt more strongly through the words written in *Le Vice-Consul* and in the text of *India Song.* One reads in *India Song:*

> Des larmes sur le visage de la femme. . .
> Elle pleure. Sans souffrance.
> Etat de pleurs. . . .

Voix I

> Ne souffre pas n'est-ce pas. . . ?

Voix II

> Non plus.
> Une lèpre, du coeur.

Voix I

Ne supporte pas. . . ?

Voix II

Non.
Ne supporte pas.
Les Indes, ne supporte pas. (IS, 33-34)

And again even more directly described:

—On la dirait . . . prisonnière d'une sorte de
souffrance. Mais . . . très ancienne. . . trop
ancienne pour encore l'attrister . . . Temps.

Pourtant elle pleure . . . Des gens l'ont vue. . .
dans le parc . . . quelquefois . . . .
(IS, 71)

Charles Rossett remarks her tears:

. . . il voit tout à coup, voilà, c'est vrai, les larmes.

. . . Il lui semble se souvenir que dans l'exil du regard de l'ambassadrice, depuis le commencement de
la nuit il y avait des larmes qui attendaient le matin.
(VC, 164)

And, at last, the woman-object explains her tears and her role:

Je pleure sans raison que je pourrais vous dire, c'est
comme une peine qui me traverse, il faut bien que
quelqu'un pleure, c'est comme si c'était moi. (VC,
198)

As Mieke Bal briefly notes in "Un roman dans le roman:" "Elle seule
montre—et peut montrer . . . la tristesse profonde qui est refoulée
par les autres."[13]
    The reader recognizes this level of the Anne-Marie Stretter para-

digm more quickly than does the film viewer. On the screen we see
the motionless, staring woman. We may, but do not certainly, recognize the tears in her eyes. And we hear the noises of Calcutta and
the cries and songs of the beggarwoman in the background. In *Le
Vice-Consul* we read these objective correlatives of her feelings at
the times of her tears or statue-like poses, and so become more
surely aware of her significance:

> Sur les talus, partout, s'égrènent, en files indiennes,
> des chapelets de gens aux mains nues. . . . Des
> gens marchant, ils portent les sacs, des bidons, des
> infants ou ils ne portent rien.

> Mille sur les talus, ils transportent, posent, re-
> partent les mains vides, gens autour de l'eau vide des
> rizières . . . dix mille, partout, cent mille, partout,
> en grains serrès sur les talus ils marchent, procession
> continues, sans fin. . . .

> Fatigue.

> Ils ne parlent pas pour ne pas la réveiller. . . .
> (VC, 175-176)

That Anne-Marie Stretter symbolizes Life *and* Death follows
from this parallel with India. She is Love and India. India is the
continuum of all, in its overwhelming masses: Age/Youth, Wealth/
Poverty, Horror/Beauty, Life/Death. India is the paradox, expressed
by characters both acting and described, of life in death (Anne-Marie
Stretter, the whites of India, the attaché), and of death in life (the
Vice-consul, the beggarwoman, the lepers), and of love and yet
horror for that love (Anne-Marie Stretter, the Vice-consul, the attaché, all those who are impassioned by, but unable to bear "India"
—"ne supporte pas," "ne s'habitue pas").

Again, the parallel is clearer to the reader than to the film viewer.
During the film one hears the "Parleuses," who by the tone of voice,
hesitations, long and heavy silences, and lack of inflection, express
fear and horror on an abstracted level for the happenings of the
story. But to read the words, clearly placed on the page, leaves no
room for conjecture. The voices speak of the beggarwoman:

Les voix restent basses, apeurées.

Voix I

... n'est pas morte. ..

Voix II

Ne peut pas mourir.

Voix I (à peine)

Non . . .

Silence. (IS, 29)

And in the parallel passage in the novel, the Vice-consul describes the beggarwoman to the attaché, but aptly posits the status of them all: "La mort dans une vie en cours, . . . mais qui ne vous rejoindrait jamais? C'est ça?" (Death which is in your life but which could never join you? Is that it?) (VC, 174). Anne-Marie Stretter and the Vice-consul understand their co-identity and paradoxical relationship, and express the same inevitable fact. In *Le Vice-Consul:*

AMS: Je sais qui vous êtes, dit-elle. Nous n'avons pas besoin de nous connaître davantage. Ne vous trompez pas.
VC: Je ne me trompe pas. . . .
AMS: Je suis avec vous. (VC, 143–144)

In the text of *India Song:*

VC: Vous êtes avec moi devant Lahore. Je le sais. Vous êtes en moi. Je vous emmènerai en moi. . . .
       Je n'avais pas besoin de vous inviter à danser pour vous connaître. Et vous le savez.
AMS: Je le sais. (IS, 97)

The viewer/listener reaches broader, more abstract conclusions linking Anne-Marie Stretter, the Vice-consul, the 'India Song,' India as Life/Love/Immobility, and the contrasting Death/Love/Mobility.

84

By contrast, the reader learns details and facts and draws story-line conclusions which allow the binary opposition of various elements, finally leading to their co-identification and the creation of a continuum. The reader learns:

Anne-Marie Stretter:	vs.	Vice-consul:
white and deathlike		dark and virile
dressed in black		dressed in white
woman/adultress		man/virgin
Love		Non-Love
		(lack of physical love)

Immobility =		Mobility =
(The impossibility or fatality of action: to act, to love, would destroy her gift of soothing others' pain. Therefore, she must remain mute, immobile, silent, in tears. She must reject the active love of the vice-consul.)		(The impossibility of remaining silent. Continual wandering and crying out the anguish to sooth it. Continual and futile activity in the attempt to release himself from pain.)

Anima	> <	Animus

The final terms of the opposition show the resolution of the apparent conflict: Anne-Marie Stretter is Anima to the Vice-consul and he is Animus to her. Both are stylized representations. They are "one" and, recognizing this, they form a pact of silence.

Only at the end of *Le Vice-Consul* does Anne-Marie Stretter explain her role in words. She cannot take active interest in the Vice-consul, for she would thereby cease to be the "object" of salvation and release to all others: " . . . je ne peux pas être celle qui est là avec vous qu'en . . . perdant mon temps comme ça . . . vous voyez" (VC, 194). The viewer of *India Song* learns by observing the groupings and activities of the actors and by hearing the music, voices, and background noises:

Anne-Marie Stretter =

Object of Love (and life),	but also	Vision of death (Immobile, wearing black)
Inspires love	while being	Incapable of sharing love
Related to music and beauty,	yet also	Related to horror and fear
Life-giving source (water-related, pale and cooling)	yet	she herself is burning and unable to receive solace
Ageless-timeless,	yet at times	her beauty fades to show her old, skeletal, ugly

The Vice-Consul =

Object of hatred,	but also	Vision of life (mobile, wearing white)
Inspires horror,	yet	Shares love
Regarded with fear, pity, rejection	but	he is the only person capable of *speaking* in the film. He lives, he *acts,* he is personally involved in others' lives by feelings.
Related to music, drawn to beauty,	and also	Angered and repulsed by beauty
Death-giving source (kills lepers)	but	this act is Good. He relieves the suffering of the helpless, but cannot receive solace for his anguish.

No continuum or completion of the cycles is recognized. Since as viewers we derive a continuing series of contrasts and paradoxes, the ending of the film must be more explicit than the ending of the novel.

In the film *India Song,* to accomplish the blending of the female/male characters who are seemingly but confusingly opposed, they must appear together at the end. The Vice-consul, kneeling beside the outstretched body of Anne-Marie Stretter, silently absorbs the suffering she cannot express. She can therefore die, swimming into the cool, life-restoring sea, while continuing to live in the Vice-consul. Her death also relieves his suffering, for he cannot die. He is bound to continue to cry out his anguish against impossible existence.

In the novel *Le Vice-Consul,* the reader has already been told: "Nous sommes les mêmes," "Ne vous trompez pas," "Vous n'avez besoin de rien" (VC, 128-148 passim). One is left, then, in the ambiguity of Life/Death continuity. The story has not ended (as we recognize immediately in the film, the voices retelling the story which "happened" in the distant past)—nor will it ever end. Charles Rosset imagines a version of Anne-Marie Stretter swimming "that night," and he wonders if the Vice-consul killed himself "that night," while we read that the Vice-consul was trading stories with the Director of the European Circle back in Calcutta. Since the identification is clear (Anne-Marie Stretter=Vice-consul), these mini-versions serve the purpose of the distant voices in the film—to indicate future versions of the story and the impossibility of a definitive ending or of a definitive point of view.

As a final mention of comparative novel/film technique, we refer to Dean McWilliam's comment concerning atmosphere and the time-space relationship created in a film:

> Duras' method is to communicate directly by creating
> a stultifying atmosphere that is the objective correla-
> tive of her characters' spiritual torpor.[13]

This is a reference to the film *Détruire, dit-elle,* but is equally applicable to the oppressive, relentless heat evoked in both the novel and the film *Le Vice-Consul/India Song.* With the near immobility of the figures in the film, the static, posed views, the hazy hues beneath the slowly turning ventilating fans ("à une lenteur de cauchemar"), we move almost imperceptibly through this half-living world of India. In words we are told: "la fatigue," "cette chaleur," "la chaleur décourage," "presque rien n'est possible aux Indes" (IS, 33-81 passim).

Therefore, in both picture and word Duras continues to draw the reader and viewer through time at her chosen pace. In the novel it takes somewhat longer for the reader to become aware of the inner time, or timelessness, of the story, but the repetition of phrases describing the unbearable boredom, the heavy, humid heat, the cloying rose-laurel scent, the odors of citronella, of leprosy and muck, as well as the images of the nearly immobile figures whose only purpose seems to be seeking breath, relief from the oppressive weight of "the air," accomplish the near-stopping of time.

In the film version, the director's technique functions as accurately described by McWilliams in the same article:

> . . . the filmgoer moves through the narrative at the exact pace determined by the film's editor. Add to this the camera's power of focussing our attention exclusively on one or more characters and we see how the film artist can merge the time experience of the viewer outside the narrative with that of the characters within the film.[14]

In *India Song,* the film, we cannot be mistaken. From the first moments of the film we are set in past time—in "dead" time—by the voices, dead in their tone quality and in the world they see for us on the screen, presenting in their conversation the narrative background given in a novel.

And always these voices arrive from afar, "de loin," and are of an indescribable sweetness and slowness (IS, 11-12). The director's words in the screentext tell us what we, in fact, experience as the film begins:

> Au piano, ralenti, un air d'entre les deux guerres, nommé *India Song*. Il est joué tout entier et occupe ainsi le temps—toujours long—qu'il faut au spectateur, au lecteur, pour sortir de l'endroit commun où il se trouve quand commence le spectacle, la lecture. (IS,13)

By placing the viewer in the position of silently watching the reenacting of lives long-ended, the theme of Death is immediately rendered overt, while it is a latent theme in the novel, permeating the text on a level other than the direct story line. In the novel the characters are alive and are in the process of interacting to tell their story, while on the screen all are already dead—moving in silence, playing out the roles of bodies with no souls, no direction, no real lives— just as they were spiritually dead and empty during their lifetimes. The reader of the *Vice-Consul,* then, is not in the same "dead" time as is the reader/viewer of *India Song.*

We agree with Dean McWilliams to disagree with George Bluestone and Gerald Barrett, who feel that a film cannot well depict "mental states."[15] In fact, and in conclusion, Marguerite Duras uses her camera and her technical skill to render overwhelmingly apparent to the viewer what does not appear on paper in *Le Vice-Consul:* the inner state of mind of this man.

On paper, the apparently important and mysterious question of why Jean-Marc de H. killed the lepers turns out to be a banal social problem. As Mieke Bal explains: "Si l'on doit admettre que le conduite violente du vice-consul soit une réaction à la vie sous les tropiques, on est obligé d'envisager la possibilité que cette vie, à laquelle ils [la communauté blanche] se sont tous adaptés, soit inacceptable."[16] What does become mystifying, suspenseful and meaningfully involving to the reader/viewer of *India Song* is the process of identification of the two figures, Anne-Marie Stretter and the vice-consul, as made evident by the manner of their representation in the film. We participate in their states of mind as we are drawn into the oppressive "ennui" of their non-lives, through the sights and sounds of the film, to recognize the eventual unifying of the Two into One continuing spirit of Love (life), blending with Non-Love (death).

NOTES

[1] Dean McWilliams, "The Novelist as Filmmaker: Marguerite Duras' *Destroy, She Said," Literature and Film Quarterly* 3, (1975): 264–69; François Regnault, "Comme," *Cahiers Renaud Barrault* 89: 33–42.

[2] Alfred Cismaru, *Marguerite Duras* (New York: Twayne,

1971); Marguerite Duras and Xavière Gauthier, *Les Parleuses* (Paris: Minuit, 1974); Carol J. Murphy, "Marguerite Duras: le texte comme écho," *French Review* 50 (1977): 850–57.

3 Joel C. Block, "Narrative Point of View in *Le Vice-Consul* of Marguerite Duras," *Hebrew University Studies in Literature* 4 (1976):114–23; Christian Zimmer, "Dans la nuit de Marguerite Duras," *Les Temps Modernes* 26 (1969): 1309.

4 Cismaru, *Duras;* Murphy, "Echo."

5 Claude Lévi-Strauss, "La geste d'Asdiwal," *Les Temps Modernes* 15 (1961): 1080.

6 Marguerite Duras, *Le Ravissement de Lol V. Stein* (Paris: Gallimard, 1964).

7 Mieke Bal, "Un Roman dans le roman: Encadrement ou enchâssement? Quelques aspects du *Vice Consul*," *Neophilologus* 58 (1974): 12; Murphy, "Echo" 855.

8 Duras, *Le Vice-Consul* (Paris: Gallimard, 1965). Subsequent page references to this edition are indicated as (VC, page number).

9 Bal, "Un Roman dans le roman," 9.

10 Duras, *L'Amour* (Paris: Gallimard, 1972); *La Femme du Gange* (Paris: Gallimard, 1973).

11 Duras, *India Song* (Paris: Gallimard, 1974) 17. Subsequent page references to this edition are indicated with the abbreviation IS.

12 Duras, *La Femme du Gange,* 126.

13 McWilliams, "Novelist as Filmmaker," 265.

14 Duras, "Novelist as Filmmaker," 268.

15 Duras, "Novelist as Filmmaker," 268–69.

16 Bal, "Un Roman dans le roman," 9.

9. THE APOCALYPTIC MILIEU OF PYNCHON'S *GRAVITY'S RAINBOW*

Laurence Daw

MARCUS SMITH AND Khachig Tölölyan have defined *Gravity's Rainbow* as "a new Jeremiad," believing this form of apocryphal lament for the state of a fallen world, firmly established in the American tradition by the very Puritans so often described by Pynchon, to be the one most aptly contained in his largest novel.[1] The main symbol of this novel is the Rainbow, an eschatological sign representing a covenant with man which will prevent the recurrence of apocalyptic destruction. In Pynchon's novel, the Rainbow is represented by the parabola of a deadly V-2 rocket's trajectory; the symbol therefore has a dual function. The parabola is actually a figure well-suited to describe *Gravity's Rainbow* because it is comprised of two distinct parts separated by an extreme point. Topographically, the parabola is a mathematical relation comprised of two parts separated by a point of zero slope. The extreme point is a point of transformation, a changing from one degree of order to another.

Gravity's Rainbow is constructed from a series of oppositions which tend to be rather ambiguous because Pynchon never defines one pole of the opposition as "better" than the other. It is the mediation of the conflict between opposites which concerns Pynchon, not the triumph of one opposing quantity over another. As Douglas A. Mackey says, "this he calls 'the interface,' the crossroads of subject and object of perception, the locus of transformation from one state of consciousness to another. . . . Here is the tightrope that anyone wishing to know the truth must walk." Pynchon uses the shape of the parabola to show the change from one order of being to another, and he uses the idea of the interface to illustrate the possibility of resolving dualities.

Pynchon creates a Rilkean conception of life as a type of flux, a flow of Being at the interface, because on that edge are contained all possibilities. It must be stressed that although *Gravity's Rainbow* is an apocalyptic novel because it shows a world living beneath the threat of an almost metaphysical Rocket which falls without sound, it is just as much a post-apocalyptic novel because it counters the threat with the possibility of redemption.

In writing his apocalyptic novel, Pynchon also tries to write a post-apocalyptic novel. Much of *Gravity's Rainbow* speculates about what may happen after, or lie beyond, the apocalypse, as much, in fact, as is speculated about the form of the apocalypse itself. This attention to potential redemption or transcendence is not unusual for Pynchon; he is a very romantic writer. Yet, his romantic conception of the apocalypse may say something more about the nature of apocalyptic literature itself.

By examining his idea of balance in the presentation of eschatological subjects, we see how Pynchon makes the apocalypse a very romantic subject, and if we take other examples from literature such as Shelley's *Prometheus Unbound,* or look as far back as the Book of Revelation itself, we are forced to ask the question: is apocalyptic literature, by nature, essentially romantic because it must imply the post-apocalyptic state? In *Gravity's Rainbow,* the form of the text answers that question.

Since it is such a comprehensive novel, it does not shrink from carefully describing all aspects of both the holocaust and the redemption. By examining both sides of the Rainbow we see the horror of a world existing beneath the poised threat of the silent and terrible Rocket, but also see the limitless beauty of love, religious faith, and cyclical regeneration. Pynchon has created a heteromythic and heterological text in order to adequately portray the apocalypse. His idea of balance in the structure and presentation of his novel is actually derived from an older tradition of apocalyptic literature. Within the apocalyptic milieu, destruction implies redemption, the erasing of one order of being implies the creation of another, better order.

Pynchon best illustrates the impending apocalypse by means of the inversion of the Rainbow symbol which comprises the parabola of destruction traced by the V-2 rocket's trajectory. This symbol dominates the lives of many characters:

> it is a curve each of them feels, unmistakably. It is the parabola . . . everything, always, collectively, had been moving towards that purified shape latent in the sky, that shape of no surprise, no second chances, no return. Yet they do move forever under it, reserved for its own black and white bad news as certainly as if it were the Rainbow, and they its children. (209)

This black and white Rainbow is a symbol of noiseless death, its end-points described in terms of the Kabbala's Qlippoth, or "shells of the dead." It is "a shape of no return," and indicates how men are perpetually separated from the Body of God and forced to sing their jeremiad in a world awaiting its apocalypse.

Slothrop shows how men in such a world are paranoids; they exhibit what he calls "the Puritan reflex": "Slothrop can feel this beast in the sky: its visible scales and claws are being mistaken for clouds and other plausibilities . . . or else everyone has agreed to *call them other names* when Slothrop is listening" (241). As the so-called "Parable of the Body Cells" suggests, the idea of a return to innocence, to a life without the Puritan reflex, is reduced to the status of a fiction:

> It's been a prevalent notion. Fallen sparks. Fragments of vessels broken at the Creation. And someday, somehow, before the end, a gathering back to home. A messenger from the Kingdom, arriving at the last moment. But I tell you there is no such message, no such home—only the millions of last moments . . . no more. Our history is an aggregate of last moments. (149)

In fact, innocence is shown to be a myth created by an evil, ruling corporate elite. The scientist Franz Pökler's abilities are entrapped at the Zwölfkinder amusement park, as the elite show him surrogate versions of his daughter Ilse: "In developing an official version of innocence, the culture of childhood has proven invaluable." (419)

93

In this fallen world, as Pynchon puts it, "Death has come in the pantry door: stands watching them, iron and patient, with a look that says *try to tickle me*." (60) As Walter Rathenau, "architect of the cartelized state" (164) says, there is "the persistence, then, of structures favouring death. Death converted into more death." (167) In creating his official version of innocence man has forgotten that, as Rathenau makes clear, "the real movement is not from death to any rebirth. It is from death to death-transfigured." (166) Slothrop sees evidence of the ultimate death-creator of the 20th century, the atomic bomb dropped on Hiroshima. It is described as an apocalyptic finger —like the Rocket—pointing down to the earth from the sky—and also as a penis, a procreative organ transformed into one of destruction: "a giant white cock, dangling in the sky straight downward out of a white pubic bush." (693) Yet, this image is countered in the novel by one which is similar, but more creative. Although the world awaits the apocalypse in *Gravity's Rainbow*—"A screaming comes across the sky. It has happened before, but there is nothing to compare it to now" (3) (the opening lines of the novel)—there is some hope for transcendence.

When Tyrone Slothrop reaches his peaceful end in the beautiful Hartz mountains, he sees a progenitive image:

> a very thick rainbow here, a stout rainbow cock driven down out of pubic clouds into Earth, green wet valleyed Earth, and his chest fills and he stands crying, not a thing in his head, just feeling natural. (626)

Within the text such a vision is not unique. The soldier Tchitcherine sees the legendary "Kirghiz light" "in a place which is older than darkness" (358), and even tiny insects in Jerusalem straw hear the voice of a Saviour "as bursts of energy from the invisible distance." (174) Slothrop also has a dream about a woman who had a womb of Bosch-like proportions and from whose "body streams now a flood of different creatures, octopuses, reindeer, Kangaroos" (447), and the aerodynamics man Fahringer brings tranquility to the rocket experiments by embracing an oriental philosophy, "out in the pine woods at Peenemünde with his Zen bow and roll of pressed straw" (403).

However, perhaps the most compelling beauty that redeems the fallen world is the love existing between Jessica and Roger Mexico.

They retreat to the English countryside to escape the War, and Beaver, Jessica's terrible fiancé who is seen as an embodiment of the War. Mexico, the probability man, describes love as "the first real data he can't argue away" (38), and allows himself to feel desire to the extent that he can say "Fuck the war." (42) When Jessica and Mexico, in undoubtedly the most beautiful scene in *Gravity's Rainbow,* take their love to the Advent services of a country church and join Preterite souls awaiting the coming of their Redeemer, Pynchon shows us a way of life "more closely belonging to Earth, to deep strata, other times." (130) The balanced shape of the parabola provides a counter to apocalyptic horror; it also allows pastoral idealism.

Therefore, *Gravity's Rainbow* is filled with both dystopias and utopias. In the novel, physical locations help to define the sources of evil forces and the opposing good counterforces. Pynchon creates a type of psychogeography where Black Magic infests certain areas and White Magic others. Evil places include the Brocken, Nordhausen, Blicheröde, the Mittelwerke, and, above all, the mythic *Raketenstadt.* Good places include the villages of the Hartz, the tropics, the plains of the Kirghiz light, and the sky, especially over places such as Lübeck or the Casino Herman Goering. Douglas Fowler sees "tropical nature" set against "the Christian North" in Pynchon's novel, in much the same way as it is in D.H. Lawrence: "North is Death's region . . . . The Rocket had to be produced out of a place called Nordhausen. The town adjoining was named Blicheröde as a validation" (322).

The dystopian portions of the psychogeography are part of "a Corporate City-State where technology was the source of power" (578) which is modelled after Fritz Lang's dystopian film *Metropolis.* Its primary symbol is the quintessential *Raketen-Stadt,* an "intimate cubic environment" (735) in which are contained the principles of "thermodynamic elitism" (677–78), the stealing of energy from others to freeze "back the tumultuous cycles of the day to preserve this odourless small world, this cube of changelessness" (678). Pynchon symbolizes the state of the city by referring to what he calls the Si-N phenomenon, taking the names of Silicon and Nitrogen from the periodic table of the elements to create the word "sin" and to evoke the Christian myth of the Fall. Pynchon refers to the chemist Kekulé's discovery of the benzene ring, which is necessary to the production of the plastics that litter the fallen gardens of the *Raketen-Stadt,* in a dream about a serpent hourobouros.

This serpent tempts man away from nature, encouraging him to create his own substances, "new molecules assembled from the debris of the given" (413).

However, the dream of a utopia is never lost in *Gravity's Rainbow*. Near its end we see young Slothrop arguing with his father about "screwing in" (698), a fantasy in which rebellious members of a youth cult pass electricity through their brains in order to create a technological utopia where they "can live forever, in a clean, honest, purified Electroworld" (699). Theirs is a truly utopian dream, but a more humane version of it is given in the description of the quaint town of Mingeborough, a country locale in the Berkshires of New England which also appears in Pynchon's short story about racism, "The Secret Integration." Tyrone Slothrop's ancestor William also calls those hills his own, and no matter where they are located such pockets of utopian idealism are the counterforce for the evil force of the *Raketen-Stadt,* and are yet another example of Pynchon's balancing technique. Apocalyptic threats are ubiquitous in *Gravity's Rainbow,* but the hope for redemption remains, and such hope is maintained because a potential exists for two kinds of leadership: evil and good.

The evil leaders in the world tending towards apocalypse suffer from what Pynchon calls "the Götterdämmerung mentality." They are, in several allusions to Wagner's *Ring Cycle* in *Gravity's Rainbow,* portrayed as denizens of the underworld, the Nibelungen of science armed with their sacred benzene ring. Trying to usurp the power of the old gods of Nature, they are doomed to fail because, following the older apocalyptic pattern, they will cause Ragnarok, the twilight of the gods.

The terrible leader of these Nibelungen is Captain Blicero. "He is the Zone's worst specter" (666), and his teeth are "long, terrible, veined with bright brown rot . . . and back in his night-breath, in the dark oven of himself, always the coiled whispers of decay." He is used to show fallen man at his absolute, sadomasochistic worst. Blicero dresses in drag, wearing false genitals made of "Mipolam, the new polyvinyl chloride" (95), and is obsessed with the decadent romanticism of Rainer Maria von Rilke, who praised the beauty of sacrificial or suicidal death. In fact, *Gravity's Rainbow* ends as Blicero's Rocket 00000 reaches the end of its fatal rainbow and destroys its living cargo, the enslaved young Gottfried. Yet, the novel ends with an unfinished phrase; fraught with potential, it is like a closed loop of film which can be run again and again. The ending of

Pynchon's novel is deliberately indeterminate because of the way it deals with the apocalypse; it must always provide a potential for reversal.

The evil leaders are, therefore, opposed throughout the novel. The title of its last section is "The Counterforce," and it is used to posit a non-deterministic model of the universe. Members of this Counterforce use a technique they call "Creative Paranoia." As Pirate Prentice says:

> Of course, a well-developed They-System is neces-
> sary—but it's only half the story. For every They
> there ought to be a We. In our case there is. Creative
> paranoia means developing at least as thorough a
> We-system as a They-system.(638)

Such a succinct description of a balance between opposing forces seems to best describe Pynchon's fictional technique in *Gravity's Rainbow* and lets us see how it is both apocalyptic and post-apocalyptic at the same time.

Pynchon always gives some sympathetic attention to the plight of the Preterite which offsets the harshness of his writing. Two stories about pigs show us "Preterite Power" in the novel. As Raketmensch, Slothrop acts in the role of "the Pig-Hero who, sometime back in the 10th century, routed a Viking invasion, appearing suddenly out of a thunderbolt and chasing a score of screaming Norsemen back into the sea" (567). The other story concerns Slothrop's famous ancestor William, who wrote *On Preterition* and took pigs to Boston in the 1600s. William associated his pigs with the Preterite souls of Puritan theology, finding a virtue in their lowliness, "possessed by an innocence they couldn't lose, by a faith in William as another variety of pig, at home with the Earth, sharing the same gift of life" (555). William seems to have the same relationship with his pigs as the Hereros do with the Erdschweinen.

The Hereros adapt their own myths to Destiny in the Zone, living in "Erdschweinhöhlen" (315) near Nordhausen to symbolize the fact that they are Preterite, like the poorest of the Hereros whose "totem animal was the Erdschwein or aardvark" (315). They are trying to recreate their fertility through the symbol of Rocket 00001, which they are assembling themselves in parallel with Blicero's Schwarzrakete 00000, because "back in Südwest, the Erdschwein-höhle was a powerful symbol of fertility and life. But here in the

97

Zone its real status is not so clear" (316). The Erdschweinhöhle project "praises and prophecies that era of innocence" (321) the young Hereros have missed, and opposes Blicheröde's Weissmann.

In the Herero community two opposing philosophies are at war, like the two sides of the parabola that the Rocket will follow. Ombindi is preaching about "the Final Zero," which is a philosophy of racial suicide. He leads "the Empty Ones" who "can guarantee a day when the last Zone-Herero will die, a final zero to a collective history fully lived. It has appeal" (318). They feel "Tribal death made sense. Christian death made none at all." (318) Enzian, on the other hand, preaches a utopian ideal, that of "the Eternal Center" which "will have no history" (318) and which will reside in a timelessness and peace. Ultimately, Enzian triumphs over the forces of racial suicide by seeking the interface. He sees that "the Eternal Centre can easily be seen as the Final Zero. Names and methods vary, but the movement towards stillness is the same" (319). The assembly of Rocket 00001 becomes the goal of the tribe rather than racial suicide and this gesture is a major triumph for the Preterite. Enzian moves against Ombindi and acts out the secret wishes of his own people.

Gravity's Rainbow emerges as a very romantic work. It deals with the holocaust and with the pastoral, with utopias and dystopias, and, finally, gives us images of leadership which have the potential to take us out of evil into good. We may conclude, therefore, by reminding ourselves that *Gravity's Rainbow* is the "perfect" apocalyptic novel because it shows all aspects of pre- and post-holocaust states. It also thus vindicates the hypothesis that apocalyptic literature is essentially romantic because it provides for the possibility of new creation emerging from destruction. As in the work of Rainer Maria von Rilke, Pynchon would have us recreate the fallen world and ascend to the realm of timeless Being of the Angels.

NOTE

[1] Thomas Pynchon, *Gravity's Rainbow* (New York: Viking Press, 1973). All page references are to this edition.

10. METONYMY AND PSYCHOLOGICAL REALISM IN AUTOBIOGRAPHY

R. Victoria Arana

NOT MANY OF US would argue with the claim that in autobiography the locus of our interest is the author, whether actual or implied. If readers could also agree that the author who is implied is not necessarily the real—the historical—writer, much that is problematic in the criticism of autobiography might clear up. But most critics of autobiography have not insisted on a distinction. Consequent theoretical confusions are, of course, attributable in part to the very definitions of the genre and to presuppositions upon which the definitions are predicated.[1] One of the troublesome assumptions, the unwitting legacy of Wayne Booth (whose topic was fiction, not autobiography), is that "though the author can to some extent choose his disguises, he can never choose to disappear."[2] For Booth, the author who cannot choose to disappear is the historical author. Like Booth, critics of autobiography have reasoned that, if the real author is always (or only) implicit, we must deduce him from the text. Thus, a highly regarded critic of autobiography permits himself to observe, with virtually no qualification, that "no matter how doubtful the facts related [by an autobiographer], the text will at least present an 'authentic' image of the man who held the pen."[3] We have not come very far from Buffon's remark, "The style is the man."[4]

Considering the critical provenance of similar formulations, it is something of a shock that critics have written so little about autobiographical style, about the figurative and syntactical (or the closer) textures of autobiographical narratives.[5] We need to remedy that negligence—not only because it will refresh our way of reading autobiographies, but also because close textual analysis (of metonyms, for example) suggests that the implied author of an autobiographical work is from one vantage point only the same "person" as its real, historical author. To confound the two is equivalent to confusing the dramatized life of a stage character with the physiology of the actor who portrays him and, thus, not to see how the illusion of reality, the effect of realism, is created. Obviously, the physiological life of the dramatic character is given, the actor's body a mere vehicle for the artistically particularized, the stylized quiddity of the artistic creation. The living and breathing actor imbues his performance with an illusion of reality. In reading autobiographies, *we* do the work of the dramatic actor. Our own mental processes flesh out the words on the page.

If the styles of autobiographies have changed in the past hundred years, it is because we all have changed. (The French philosopher Michel Foucault provocatively espoused the idea that every age unconsciously subscribes to a complex of assumptions underlying its language. We need not concur entirely with his conceptualizations to recognize the validity of his general hypothesis.)[6] Clearly, in earlier periods, cultural and personal notions (if not theories) about the way people were thought to respond to their experiences determined to a large extent the degree to which readers believed literary texts were realistic. The style we now designate as *historical realism,* we recognize, is not like the one we might call *psychological realism.*

In short, psychological realism, as I shall explain, is a style, not an ethical desideratum for the genre nor even quite a generic expectation. Whereas one of the principal givens of the dramatic character's actions has always been his creaturely reality, the principal given of the autobiographer's enterprise today is that his language should imitate more or less authentically the way we associate ideas, come to conclusions, and verbalize memories, sensations, and thoughts. After modernism altered our assumptions regarding readability, we changed. Now, if a text does not induce its reader to participate imaginatively in mental processes, the life that he reads about often remains for him flat, mere script. Because ours is a psychological age, autobiographers have found themselves challenged to imitate a culturally shared notion of reality, to present life from the perceptual angle. What specific stylistic strategies avail them? In what manner are the productions undertaken in this spirit "true to life"? How are our expectations of the genre conditioned by cultural assumptions we hardly realize we subscribe to? To answer these questions however briefly, I must begin with genre theory, describe metonymy, and explain the limitations of psychoanalytical approaches to the study of autobiographical texts. Of course, I shall have to be more suggestive than exhaustive in my treatment of the relevant materials.

In defining the genre, no one wants to do away with the criterion of "real truth to life," what Elizabeth Bruss has called the "illocutionary force" of the genre. In her words, "The audience is expected to accept [the autobiographer's] reports as true, and is free to 'check up' on them or attempt to discredit them"; and Bruss adds, "The autobiographer purports to believe in what he asserts."[7] Neither of these defining conditions suggests a distinction between the historic person-who-writes and the implied author that the text evokes in our minds. The historical author may have wished to satisfy or tease the reader's expectation of truthfulness, but only the text can accomplish that satisfaction or play the joke.

What strategies autobiographers employ to create the illusion of psychological probity I have explored at length elsewhere.[8] I found that when they succeed (paradoxically, as recent psychological studies suggest), their narratives more closely imitate modernist novels than they do the actual motion of thoughts and feelings[9] or even the transcripts of psychiatric interviews where the topic of discourse is the self and the narrator freely employs the first person.[10] Stylistic models, not the direct observation of mental processes, have shown writers the way to achieve certain sought-after effects. With these few preliminary observations, I can perhaps proceed to explain the function of metonymy in the elaboration of that style of autobiography that I am calling psychological realism.

An author's use of metonymy *(crown* for *king, White House* for *president)* is hardly ever striking, for a metonym works indirectly by suggesting a contiguous term.[11] Take, for example, this sentence from Maya Angelou's *I Know Why the Caged Bird Sings:* "Through the fly-specked screen door, I could see that the arms of Momma's apron jiggled from the vibrations of her humming."[12] The metonym *apron jiggled* for "Momma hummed so loud that she shook" functions less as understatement than as a means of training our vision precisely on the images that our narrator claims to have seen and wants us to see as well. When I say, "Yesterday, on our walk in the mountains, we came across trilliums," even if no more description than that is given—a forest, early springtime, and a certain density of undergrowth are only a few of the images evoked more or less metonymically.

A metonym is a very exact sort of descriptive shorthand. When Maya Angelou writes, "The dirt of the girls' cotton dresses continued on their legs, feet, arms, and faces to make them all of a piece,"[13] as readers, we are directed to follow the trajectory of the narrator's vision, focusing on the precise subjects of her regard and feeling the virulent projection of her hatred as if its realization were generated in ourselves. Visualizing the girls' "legs, feet, arms," what we see is that these *are* dirt, "all of a piece" with the dirt on the dresses. One more brief excerpt, this one from Émile Zola's *Nana:* "The gentlemen blinked, bewildered by this decadence of petticoats whirling at the foot of the narrow stair."[13] The words *petticoats whirling* replace (perhaps even sublimate) the related ones, *women dancing.* To use a metonym as no more than stylistic embellishment would be to create no greater effect than that of preciosity.

But what Zola, in fiction, and Angelou, in her autobiography, both accomplish is quite other than precious. For them and for many writers aiming for realistic representation of experience, the metonym functions far more subtly and organically than as mere decoration. This is so because, as François Moreau has observed, "The metonym introduces no representation foreign to the isotopy and appears only, in most cases, as a simplified vision of reality."[14] The metonym belongs to the same perceptual field as the term replaced. Both terms, furthermore, are syntactically equivalent. The conciseness of the metonym produces unquestionably, as Moreau noted, "a simplified vision."

At this point, we must consider carefully the nature of that simplification in order to dispel a frequent misconception about autobiographical narratives. In psychoanalytical writings, largely due to the influence of Freudian thought on the theories of Jacques Lacan, debate is ongoing about the similarities and differences between metaphoric and metonymic signification in the dreams and the oral productions of psychiatric patients. Psychoanalysts interpret the use of metaphors and metonyms (viewed as condensed modes of periphrases) as if they were always symptoms of a repression or a disavowal, and they decode the so-called "unconscious intentional-ization" of such images.[15] If we were approaching an autobiograph-ical text for the purposes of psychiatric speculation, we would not need to limit our analysis of sublimation to its occurrence in meto-nyms or synechdoches, metaphors or symbols. As psychoanalysts, we can always prudently ignore what the patient claims is important to him; we engage him in probing his discourse. But when we sab-otage the overtly manipulative intentions of a writer by interpreting his metonyms as expressive of unconscious motives, we do him—and literary study—no service. Indeed, we often simply cheat our-selves of the pleasures the text offers us.

Needless to say, students of literature also recognize the im-portance of intention in discourse; indeed, they are far more likely than psychoanalysts to allow that, to a certain extent, the author consciously intends the effects he produces, particularly if those ef-fects result from the use of tropes. Appreciative readers justifiably assume that the writer is largely willful in expressing himself, his vision of reality. Moreau speaks representatively for many others in asserting that "what characterizes a point of style is the presence of *intention,*" especially when he goes on to say that

> intention is not necessarily esthetic; an image, we have noted, can be beautiful even though beauty is not the sought-after goal of its creator (it can have a satiric, a comic, indeed a didactic function, etc.). But it is literary because it is invested with an intention, whatever it may be (and in that case, even a cliché can become literary, provided that the writer makes voluntary use of it, so as to produce a precise effect).[16]

In his autobiography *Safe Conduct,* Boris Pasternak condensed the point: "In art the man is silent and the image speaks."[17] A writer like himself is silent, Pasternak suggests, only because he is content to let his images speak for him, because he is satisfied that the author which his words imply is the very self he intends to communicate. When Pasternak evokes the faculty at the University of Moscow in 1900 by using a metonym, we see that "there, surreptitiously, the varnished smiles of a decrepit order of things leered at one another,"

103

and we need not be told in denotative language the young poet's opinion of his would-be teachers.[18]

Metonymic expression in autobiography has its drawbacks—beyond asking us to determine whether the intention that framed it was conscious or not. Foremost, the autobiographical world evoked metonymically is filled out only to the degree that, as readers, we are familiar with that world. We need to know something about the wildflower trillium before we can compose its woodland context. Most importantly, the process of our interpretation follows a closely guided process of visualization. Those two processes, especially "seeing," may seem entirely natural; indeed, we usually do supply gestalts for desultory images, every day and all the time. Just as the actor's vitality underlies the life of the dramatic character he impersonates, our experiences of both life and literature—as I have suggested—underlie our experience of the work.

Because metonymy is perceptual and because metonyms rarely announce themselves as literary artifice, we may fail to notice how a work which seems to have psychological probity achieves its effect. Our selection of one detail in our field of vision over another is often unremarked in our lives. No wonder that so little attention is paid to metonymic imagery—especially in prose, and more especially still in autobiographies, where the narrator's perceptual eccentricity may be excused as an authentic manifestation of his special subjectivity and dismissed from further consideration, psychological or stylistic. Nevertheless, metonymy is a figure of particular usefulness to autobiographers who mean to represent not the objectified histories of their progress through life (I am thinking of works like Anthony Trollope's *An Autobiography)* but, rather, intensely subjective revisions of their formative experiences and mature lives.

In autobiography, metonymic narration can be highly suggestive in a number of ways; its details (the metonyms themselves), selected as foci of the subject's personal attention, accumulate into a skillful design of images that deliberately excludes overt reference to what might be considered communal knowledge, shared by author and reader. No writer can intelligibly sustain a web made entirely of metonyms, but he can rely heavily on them; and, when he does, that reliance creates (1) the impression of an intense and highly subjective fabric of experiences, (2) the confluence of the writer's remembrance and of the reader's literary experience, and (3) most important, the illusion that the experience narrated is psychologically realistic. As one French linguist observed when modernism was all the rage, metonymy "foreshortens distances to facilitate the rapid intuition of things already known."[19]

Other methods of spatializing a narrative have been for decades the concern of literary scholars seeking to characterize modernist fiction,[20] and so we may be exempt from reviewing them here. To my knowledge, no one has explored the uses to which the metonym has been put in creating the illusion of psychological realism in autobiography. Michel Aucouturier has studied metonymy in Pasternak's early fiction; but there the trope accomplishes quite different ends.[21] Far more relevant to my point here than the well-known catalogues of stylistic features in modernist novels and short stories —their streams of consciousness, self-reflexive narrators, poetic patternings of images, disjunctive narrative sequences, free association of ideas and so on—are the seminal studies by phenomenologists like Maurice Merleau-Ponty.[22] He, for example, observed that "objects which do not belong to the circle of the perceived exist in the sense in which truths do not cease to be true when I am not thinking of them: their mode of being is one of logical necessity and not of 'reality.'"[23] By centering on and naming only the pertinent attributes of things peripherally acknowledged to be there, autobiographers imitate our idea of psychological reality, not the reality itself. But, saturated as we are with Freudian theory—psychoanalytic notions of interior spaces, of associative and paratactic dynamisms, and so forth—we need to guard ourselves assiduously from responding emotionally and unquestioningly to a text which is seductive in a psychomodernist manner as if it were truer and so better than another text otherwise organized.

Let us look closely at the metonyms in a passage from *Safe Conduct,* a passage in which Pasternak evokes the way recruits were sent off to war in May 1914. Beatrice Scott's translation admirably reproduces Pasternak's syntax and images. In section VII, we come upon the following:

> This lamentation, which continued only for the first few months, was wider than the grief of the young wives and the mothers which was poured into it. It was ushered onto the line in perfect order. The stationmasters touched their caps as it passed them by, the telephones made way for it. *It transformed the*

district, was everywhere visible, . . . because it was an unaccustomed thing of burning brightness which had lain untouched since wars gone by. They had taken it from a secret place during the previous night and brought it behind the horses to the [train] station in the morning, and after they had led it out by the hand from the station porch they would carry it back along the bitter mud of the village road. That was how they saw the[ir] men off who were going as single volunteers. . . .

But soldiers in ready marching order passing straight into the horror itself were seen off without commotion. With everything strapped on they jumped unpeasant-like from the high railway trucks onto the sand, jingling their spurs and trailing behind them through the air their overcoats which were thrown on anyhow [any which way]. Others stood in the wagons at the cross-beams patting the horses, which stamped the dirty woodwork of the rotting floor with the proud beats of their hooves. The platform did not give away free apples, did not search its pocket for an answer, but flushing crimson laughed into the corners of tightly pinned kerchieves.[24]

The first sentence establishes a subject, lamentation. Implicit only are all those besides "the young wives and the mothers" who are lamenting. In the second through fifth sentences of Scott's translation (Pasternak's clauses are not punctuated identically), the pronoun *it* stands for the noun *lamentation.* Here the verbs (for instance, *was ushered* in the second sentence of our text) confirm that the lamentation is embodied in people, to whom the syntax does not refer as such. Because the rather vague metonym *lamentation* stands for everybody (and everything) participating in these farewells, we are forced to conjure a blurry mass of weeping souls that stationmasters and even telephone poles must give way to. When the author attributes qualities like "burning brightness" to it, we are compelled suddenly to emend our perceptions, to see the emotion as very nearly a concrete thing, something which can be "taken . . . from a secret place," "brought behind horses," "led out by the hand," and carried "along the bitter mud." We can form no very clear images of the people peripherally acknowledged to be present. Even *the mud* is a metonym (as we soon learn) for *village roads*. The beginning of the following paragraph modulates from metonymic expression to fairly straightforward description—still, however, intensely figural. Except for the word *horror*—a metonym for the bloody war—the paragraph is free from indirection until the last sentence. When we get to it, it flips us. Is *the platform* a metonym for people on the platform, or is it a vivid stratagem for eliciting irony, an absence altogether (if not of people, then of human sympathy). The ambiguity is rich but not resolvable. The last predicate ("but flushing crimson laughed") is visualizable and explicitly aural but, to me, entirely too richly suggestive to be decoded (to be deciphered) with certainty. As a whole, we probably agree, the passage impresses upon us the sense of having experienced a series of intensely idiosyncratic perceptions arranged, it would appear, to simulate a historical person's experience. But whose? The lamentation, we are told, "transformed the district, was everywhere visible." The metonymic strategy makes conspicuous to our minds that which could not have been conspicuous to an actual observer. By means of a combination of stylistic devices, including metonyms, our experience of May 1914 is brought in line with the visionary one of the autobiography's implied author. It probably does not take long before we recognize that what at first strikes us as psychologically real (a transcript of mentation) is psychological realism, a stylistically achieved illusion.

What can we safely deduce about the history of Boris Pasternak the man? About his actual experience? Not much. Only that he managed to fashion a means of asserting control over the nature of our experience while simultaneously reconstructing his own. According to those critics who have defined autobiography, *Safe Conduct* belongs to that genre so long as we are convinced that the author believes what he asserts. The issue of belief, however, is not a literary one. The historical self that projected the autobiographical persona is largely out of reach in this text.

Nevertheless, by analyzing such stylistic devices as metonyms, readers may formulate valid opinions about another, eminently literary, issue—the artistic skill of the writer. We might do worse than to conclude that the actual and the implied authors of an autobiography merge into a single identity *exclusively* in their capacities as craftsmen. We shall not, however, appreciate that merger if we do not approach the text with fairly refined sensibilities and a deep respect for the stylistic analysis of literary works.

NOTES

[1] See, for example, Elizabeth Bruss, *Autobiographical Acts* (Baltimore: Johns Hopkins University Press, 1976) 6–11; also, Louis A. Renza, "A Theory of Autobiography," in *Autobiography: Essays Critical and Theoretical,* ed. James Olney (Princeton: Princeton University Press, 1981), esp. 291, where Renza defines autobiography as "a unique, self-defining mode of self-referential expression, one that allows, then inhibits, its ostensible project of self-representation, of converting oneself into the present promised by language."

[2] Wayne Booth, *The Rhetoric of Fiction* (New York: Chicago University Press, 1961) 20.

[3] Jean Starobinski, "The Style of Autobiography," in *Autobiography: Essays Critical and Theoretical,* 75.

[4] George-Louis Leclerc de Buffon (1707–1789) in *Discours sur le Style:* "Le style est l'homme même."

[5] In "The Style of Autobiography," Starobinski says style is an interpersonal strategy, arguing that "style [in autobiography] assumes the dual function of establishing the relation between 'the author' and his past, but also, in its orientation toward the future, of revealing the author to his future readers," 74. But Starobinski's discussion is a free-wheeling exploration not of composition or rhetoric but of what he calls "stylistic tonalities"—the elegaic and the picaresque.

[6] Michel Foucault, *L'Archéologie du savoir* (Paris, 1969); in English, *The Archeology of Knowledge,* trans. A. M. Sheridan Smith (New York, 1972).

[7] Bruss, 11.

[8] For related discussion of this topic, see my article "The Psychoaesthetics of Autobiography,"*Biography: An Interdisciplinary Quarterly,* 5, 1 (Winter 1983) 53–67.

[9] See Richard Nisbett and Timothy DeCamp Wilson, "Telling More than We Can Know: Verbal Reports on Mental Processes," *Psychological Review,* 84, 3 (May 1977): 231; also Richard Nisbett

108

and Lee Ross, *Human Inference: Strategies and Shortcomings of Social Judgment* (Englewood Cliffs, New Jersey: Prentice-Hall, Inc., 1980).

[10] See James E. Gorney, "The Field of Illusion in Literature and the Psychoanalytical Situation," *Psychoanalysis and Contemporary Thought,* 2 (1979): 546.

[11] This is the standard definition given in all dictionaries and handbooks of literary terms.

[12] Maya Angelou, *I Know Why the Caged Bird Sings* (New York: Bantam Books, 1980) 25.

[13] Angelou, 25.

[14] Émile Zola, *Nana* (Paris: Bibliographie de la Pléiade, t. II) 1226: "Ces messieurs clignaient les paupières, ahuris par cette dé-gringolade de jupes tourbillonnant au pied de l'étroit escalier."

[15] François Moreau, "Métonymie et synecdoque," in *L'Image littéraire: Position du Problème* (Paris: Société d'Edition d'Enseignement Superieur, 1981) 81: "L'image métonymique n'introduit aucune représentation étrangère l'isotopie et apparâit seulement, dans la plupart des cas, comme une vision simplifiée de la realité."

[16] See discussion of this subject in Anthony Wilden's notes to Jacques Lacan, *Speech and Language in Psychoanalysis* (Baltimore: Johns Hopkins University Press, 1968) 243; also Lacan's text, esp. 13 and 15.

[17] Moreau, 100; my translation.

[18] Boris Pasternak, *Safe Conduct* (1931; New York: New Directions, 1958) 55.

[19] Pasternak 31.

[20] Gaston Esnault, *L'Imagination populaire, métaphores occidentales* (Paris: Presses Universitaires Françaises, 1925) 30–31; my translation.

[21] One early study along these lines is Joseph Frank's "Spatial Form in Modern Literature," *Sewanee Review,* 53 (1945): 221–40, 433–56; another is Ralph Freedman's *The Lyrical Novel* (Princeton: Princeton University Press, 1967).

[22] Michel Aucouturier, "The Metonymous Hero, or the Beginnings of Pasternak as a Novelist," *Books Abroad* (Spring 1970): 222–27.

[23] See, for instance, his *Phenomenology of Perception* (trans. Colin Smith; London: Routledge and Kegan Paul, 1962) and *The Structure of Behavior* (1942; New York: Beacon Press, 1963).

[24] *The Structure of Behavior,* 212.

[25] *Safe Conduct* , 108–09. I have supplied the emphasis in the first paragraph. I am indebted to Professor Josephine Z. Woll of the Department of German-Russian, Howard University, for going over this and other passages in the Russian-language text, providing the alternate translations here entered in square brackets, and sharing with me her thoughts about what I have written on this passage.

11. THE APOCALYPTIC VISION IN NATHANAEL WEST'S *MISS LONELYHEARTS*

Walter Poznar

OF APOCALYPTIC VISIONS IN the twentieth century, we have surely had enough to numb the heart and unsettle the nerves. Of these visions, none in American fiction has been as devastating, as overpowering, as Nathanael West's, for West's vision is not a simple repudiation of the spiritual barrenness of the American dream but a deadlier vision that makes the work of Steinbeck, Farrell, and others in the thirties and later seem shallow by comparison. West's tragic picture of the nature of man is clearly indebted to the profound exploration of human needs and motives in Dostoevsky but lacks Dostoevsky's sustaining faith in a Father Zossima. While Dostoevsky believed that there is, in almost all human beings, a striving for purity, a reaching out to something higher and nobler, West concluded that the disease of life makes aspiration impossible and exposes the essential sterility of the human consciousness. Where other American writers have tended to see in human nature a baffled but healthy impulse toward wholeness and community, West sees nothing but emptiness and apathy and cheap dreams. Human nature is not a battlefield on which the sordid and the beatific struggle for supremacy, but an ashen waste, like that in *The Great Gatsby,* where movement exists without direction.

While other writers have criticized contemporary society for its blatant materialism, its suppression of individual needs, and its enervating anonymity, West penetrates into the inner sanctum of the human soul and finds nothing but emptiness and childish illusions. His nihilism is neither political nor ideological nor historical but intensely private and irremediable, for when West looks at human beings he discovers nothing but pettiness and a vacant stare. His characters are ghosts, spiritless and mundane, without the heroic appetite of old Karamazov or the passion for justice of Ivan Karamazov. Neither heroism nor satanism can redeem his characters from the dreary pointlessness of their lives because there is nothing in them powerful enough to challenge or defy life. The Byronic passion that swept Europe in the early nineteenth century and penetrated even into the remote corners of Russian society has spent its force, has lost its nerve and lapsed into quietism. There are no more Eugene Onegins or Vautrins left, for West's characters are mired in spiritual apathy: they no longer question life or seek to redeem themselves or even question the world they inhabit. They are no longer seekers in this sense, but stereotyped victims.

Man receives in West's fiction his final judgment, the ultimate revelation that there is nothing to seek and no reason to grow, that there are no gods, no ideals, no reasons for anger, no causes to espouse, no private self into which one may retreat and live in comparative contentment. Man cannot, like Montaigne, retire to the country and explore the inner recesses of his private consciousness and the condition of mankind. There is no past to which man can return, as Charles Lamb did, to find beauty and peace of mind, a private shelter from a degraded present. Nor can he resolve his confusion by adopting the tempered and ironic detachment of an Anatole France.

Even the tormented, nightmarish visions of an Andreyev are denied him, while the sentimental pietism of a Steinbeck is too ludicrous and irrelevant to contemplate. Tedious psychological exploration of the individual consciousness has become a childish game, a charade, a futile toying with disembodied concepts and infantile illusions. Nowhere in West's fiction is this ultimately nihilistic vision so overpowering as in his short novel *Miss Lonelyhearts* (1933), in some respects the most tragic novel in modern American fiction. What West rejects in the novel is virtually every form of consolation and psychological fantasy man is capable of. Within its brief narrative span, the work is as unrelenting in its corrosive satire as *Candide,* but without Voltaire's humor and the redemptive solace

Voltaire offers at the conclusion—the advice to cultivate one's own garden and thereby find peace of mind.

West rejects all forms of hedonism as essentially spiritless and absurd. Miss Lonelyhearts' encounter with Fay Doyle in his room is a dismal and enervating experience. His pursuit of Shrike's wife is a farcical soap opera, for even were he to achieve his objective, there is little doubt it would be as dreary as every other sexual success he has had. Betty, who loves him, is beyond his reach, for "her sureness was based on the power to limit experience arbitrarily."[1] Betty tells him "that he ought to live there in the country and that if he did, he would find that all his troubles were city troubles" (106). Even their trip to the country solves nothing for Miss Lonelyhearts, for "although spring was well advanced, in the deep shade there was nothing but death—rotten leaves, gray and white fungi, and over everything a funereal hush" (119). The pleasures of drinking and brawling are no less sterile because they lead nowhere and leave an appalling hangover of the spirit. The lure of money and success has long since lost its appeal. The world of idealism is far too tenuous and abstract to mean anything, while the comfort offered by art never really touches the spirit or lasts.

It is Shrike, in the early part of the novel, who systematically and brutally itemizes the forms of refuge to which Miss Lonelyhearts might retire, each to Shrike pathetically unworthy of serious consideration. One cannot, like Gauguin, escape the human condition by fleeing to the South Seas or achieve real paralysis of the soul in sensualism. What is inescapable is the merciless logic of Shrike's withering sarcasm, for Miss Lonelyhearts knows Shrike is right, Shrike his alter ego, that inner voice he struggles to deny. Like Dmitri Karamazov, he tries to resolve the chaos within his soul, but he lacks Dmitri's innocence, his genuine power of love, and his innate humility.

It is *The Brothers Karamazov* that stands, in the novel, as a terrifying reminder of what was once possible, a realm of being and seeking and believing that the contemporary world has long since desecrated. In the lacerated world of West's novel, there are no counterparts of Alyosha, Father Zossima, Ivan, even old Karamazov. What Alyosha tells the children at the conclusion of the novel no longer makes any sense, is spiritually impossible because the ashen waste of the modern spirit is irredeemable. The passage on love he reads in *The Brothers Karamazov* would, if followed, help the world to learn to love, but Miss Lonelyhearts knows that this beautiful passage is meaningless today.

"As a boy in his father's church, he had discovered that something stirred in him when he shouted the name of Christ, something secret and enormously powerful. He had played with this thing, but had never allowed it to come alive" (75). The agony of guilt and shame and repentance, the miracle of spiritual rebirth, and the sublime innocence of love in *The Brothers Karamazov* are subjected to savage mockery in West's novel, all the more savage and bitter because they once conferred meaning and vitality on life. A Grand Inquisitor would be as ineffectual and anachronistic in contemporary society as the kiss Jesus confers on the old man. No cosmic drama exalts man's fate. Only sordid fragments remain of the grandeur with which man confronted destiny in classical literature. Everything is on a smaller, pettier scale, as becomes clear in the letters Miss Lonelyhearts receives. The age of the mass man has arrived, dominated, particularly in America, by the pervasiveness of banal stereotypes and gratuitous violence and the numbing isolation of the individual. Only the Hollywood dream world is left, the vapid mannequins that simulate vitality and virility and compassion and the healthy exuberance of a Falstaff or a Rabelais. As Jay Martin notes in his book on West, in West's short story "Mr. Potts of Pottstown," Potts discovers that "there is no real life to which Potts can awaken—only a collective dream life in which dream feeds on dream, monstrously."[2] And these dreams, so objectively delineated in *The Day of the Locust,* are as stiff and flavorless as wax fruit, created not out of the rich unconsciousness of a private soul, but out of advertising copy.

Were Jesus alive today, West implies, no one would even trouble to crucify him because he poses no danger to anyone. The emasculation of Jesus in contemporary culture runs parallel to the emasculation of the Devil, for both have been tamed, rendered banal, so unsubstantial as embodiments of higher truths that they are indistinguishable from the papier-mâché cultural idols of a decadent world. If Miss Lonelyhearts does, as West once suggested, become "the portrait of a priest of our time who has a religious experience,"[3] then that experience is neither expressed nor rendered effective in the insane world in which he lives. The little park to which he repairs is a pathetic reminder of what nature itself might once have been, an enduring symbol of rebirth and joy and passion, but the park is now little more than a shriveled and desiccated patch of ground struggling desperately to give birth to some form of green life. It is as barren as the religious vision Miss Lonelyhearts has at the end. Whatever of Prince Myshkin there may be in Miss Lonelyhearts, it is tainted and corrupted by the poison of its own frenzied frustration and inability to ennoble itself. To feel the pain of life, to feel, as Miss Lonelyhearts does, the crushing reality of the suffering expressed so clumsily but so poignantly in the letters that arrive each day, is to succumb to the monstrous rage of an Ivan Karamazov, a fate Miss Lonelyhearts strives to overcome at the conclusion, only to rush headlong into the silence of death.

Man cannot be redeemed—that is perhaps the most crushing reality in West's universe, for to be redeemed there must be some seed of nobility, some purity of soul, some Promethean fire, some power of love as in Zossima, a spiritual vision, a Byronic spirit that refuses to bend in subjection or to renounce its innate integrity. The fortuitousness of experience and passion, the haphazard flashing of individual needs and emotions, and the barbaric force of violence are realities that devastate man's need to vindicate himself, to believe in the worth of the private consciousness, to receive the gift of being in joy and quiet faith. Even the impulse of compassion can be suddenly transformed into anger: "Miss Lonelyhearts felt as he had felt years before, when he had accidentally stepped on a small frog. Its spilled guts had filled him with pity, but when its suffering had become real to his senses, his pity had turned to rage and he had beaten it frantically until it was dead" (87). Only once in the novel is there a fleeting intimacy when the hands of the cripple Doyle and of Miss Lonelyhearts touch: "At first the cripple covered his embarrassment by disguising the meaning of the clasp with a handshake, but he soon gave in to it and they sat silently, hand in hand" (126). One is reminded of those rare moments of brotherhood celebrated by Silone in his novels.

This nihilistic vision in West's novel has its roots in man's nature, not in social systems or political ideologies or psychological discoveries about the underside of man's consciousness. Ethical philosophers throughout the ages have wrestled with the same problem in order to rescue man from himself, but nothing in the modern age can rescue man because, shorn of all his traditional ideals and grandiose visions of himself, he stands as a being bereft of every consoling grace, a cipher, maudlin beyond imagining, pathetic beyond description, trapped like Sartre's dramatic protagonists in a hell from which there is no exit. The suggestion by Sophocles that it would be better not to have been born underscores the anguish of being alive. Perhaps the controlled balance of his plays renders that message all the more shattering, for the Apollo of art has ordered and harmonized a vision of life that is implacably dark and pointless. What in West's world do men have to offer one another? What gift can they give that will touch the spirit and strengthen the will? What does Miss Lonelyhearts have to offer, even out of his realization that suffering is real? His symbolic gesture at the end is as ineffectual and as cruel as would be a gesture offered the bleeding Oedipus.

The most tragic message in West's novel is that human beings have so precious little to offer in the way of kindness, understanding, strength. What can Miss Lonelyhearts offer to Betty? Or to the cripple Doyle? Or to anyone? Where man once turned to divine powers for those sacred offerings that would cleanse life and lift the spirit, he must now look to himself, for nowhere outside of himself is there a ministering angel or a guardian deity to soothe his anxiety or lighten the awesome burden of isolation. When Aldous Huxley passed through California in the twenties, as he records in his book *Jesting Pilate,* he could find nothing but cheap glamour and crass sentimentalism, what West discovered in his years in Hollywood. Listen to Jay Martin's account of West's first day at Republic Studios:

> His first day at Republic, dressed in a reddish Norfolk jacket, he was assigned to share an office with Lester Cole at the rear of the studio, with windows overlooking some trees. West immediately recognized that the birds there were shrikes—butcherbirds, killers of other birds—and was "terribly angered." He had, to Cole's astonishment, "a particularly intense hatred for this bird," and "the next day he brought an air rifle to the studio and spent half the day killing them."[4]

But West knew that the shrike that preys on man's heart is a demon that cannot be killed. And the Miss Lonelyhearts of the world are left to agonize over their own impotence, unable to cool the fever of rage and resentment that consumes the soul. For even what is pure and beautiful is contaminated by the venomous canker in man's heart, as the decomposing body of Father Zossima is taken by some as evidence of Zossima's impurity and unholy life. Alyosha is powerless to counteract the suspicion that hangs over Zossima's moldering corpse. The demon of disbelief is rooted implacably in man's soul and there is no way to exorcise it. If Zossima fails, if Prince Myshkin fails, how can a Miss Lonelyhearts reach the soul?

What redeems West's bleak indictment of human nature is the weight of sorrow in Miss Lonelyhearts, not the easy sentimentalism of pious clichés, but the aching sense of loneliness and fear West himself felt throughout his life. Like Alyosha, there was in Nathanael West a sorrow for mankind that never demeans itself or others, a spiritual quality Dostoevsky would have understood, an integrity of pain and humanness that communicated itself to those West associated with. Leonard Fields observed that "it wasn't in a mercenary manner that Nate met these people, because they would sense that . . . he didn't want to meet people to use them *at all*. He never used anybody. He met them because he liked them. And in liking him, they automatically offered him things."[5] It is the quality we recognize in Alyosha, an aura of decency and respect, that simple purity of the spirit that can never desecrate the sanctity of the private consciousness. Though everything West saw only confirmed his painful sense of what is cheap and degrading and cruel in human nature, he never abandoned his innate integrity, his respect for what man must endure and suffer. He was never beguiled by ideology into believing that social planning and technology would ever assuage that inner feeling of aloneness and pain he felt so intensely. What Shelley called "the giant agony of the world" was not for West a peevish stereotype, an abstract concept, a churlish form of self-pity to excuse one's own shortcomings and inadequacies, but an ineluctable reality. One comes close to West's sense of life in Jerome Chodorov's comment that "he was a skeptic, but a hopeful one . . . . He didn't really believe mankind could save itself . . . by politics or any other thing—but was trying hard to believe it."[6] Against the hard logic of human experience and the innate skepticism of his own nature, West refused to concede defeat and maintained the strength of his own intuitive need to belive in life. Like those tragic writers who in the conflict of life depict their protagonists going down to defeat but can never relinquish their belief in the struggle, West managed, like Ishmael in *Moby-Dick,* to survive as a human being.

In the final analysis, West could never have accepted the studied influence of a Vonnegut, the crass sensationalism of a Burroughs, the obsession with violence of a Joyce Carol Oates, the tepid sentimentalism of a Steinbeck, the crude macho image of a Hemingway, the vaporous mysticism of a Salinger, or the convoluted cynicism of a Pynchon. He remains in our literature as a figure of generous and indomitable feelings who confronted the specter of madness and fear, yet never yielded to the hallucinatory vision of an Andreyev or the madness of a Nietzsche. He looked into the void and traveled into the depths of Dante's Inferno without ever finding Purgatorio and Paradiso, refusing the political slogans of his time and the facile pessimism of so many of our American novelists. He wrote not to judge mankind but to record its agonies and its suffering. He knew that the Candide-like experiences of Lemuel Pitkin in *A Cool Million* touched only the surface of life because West was not a Voltaire, a sturdy *philosophe* of the eighteenth century. He knew that the sardonic revelation of human hypocrisy, the clever and witty unmasking of human folly and vanity practiced so brilliantly by Sinclair Lewis, left the painful tragedy of life untouched. Where Melville in *The Confidence Man* exposed the sordid motives that inspire most people, West penetrated more deeply into the tormented soul of man. What Melville wrote of Hawthorne in "Hawthorne and His Mosses" can be as appropriately applied to West. In Hawthorne, Melville found "such a depth of tenderness, such a boundless sympathy with all forms of being, such an omnipresent love, that we must needs say that this Hawthorne is here almost alone in his generation,—at least, in the artistic manifestation of these things." The apocalyptic vision in West is as profound as Conrad's, for both writers refused to despair of man though both insisted on exploring to its roots the essential character of human experience. It is in this type of illustrious company that West belongs—whatever differences of style and technique and structure may exist—for if there is anything that unites the great tragic writers in the world's literature, it is this unshakable and clear-sighted respect for man, a respect all the more stubborn and unyielding because it has plumbed the depths, tasted the acridness of man's pain, yet preserved its own humanity and its own sweetness.

118

NOTES

[1] *The Complete Works of Nathanael West* (New York: Farrar, Straus and Cudahy, 1957) 79. All page references are to this edition.

[2] Jay Martin, *Nathanael West: The Art of His Life* (New York: Farrar, Straus and Giroux, 1970) 170.

[3] Martin, 191.

[4] Martin, 276–77.

[5] Martin, 356n.

[6] Martin, 389.

INDEX